Antique Trunks

Identification & Price Guide

Paul Pat Morse and Linda Edelstein

Published by

krause publications
An F&W Publications Company

700 E. State Street, Iola, WI 54945-0001
Telephone: 715-445-2214
www.krause.com

Please call or write for our free catalog of publications. Our toll-free number to place an order or obtain a free catalog is (800) 258-0929.

Library of Congress Catalog Number: 2003101370
ISBN: 0-87349-646-9

Edited by Dennis Thornton
Designed by Donna Mummery
Cover photography: Anne Edelstein Morse
Color photography: Anne Edelstein Morse

Manufactured in China

About the authors:

Linda Edelstein and Paul Pat Morse have been collecting and writing about antiques for more than 25 years. They have been involved with antique trunks since the mid 1970s and operated The Trunk Shop in Portsmouth, N.H., for many years. They also own and operate the Web site trunk.com, where they make available fine restored and refinished antique trunks and other practical items of distinction.

The authors have previously written two books on antique trunks, *Antique Trunks, A Time Line of Trunks*, and *Antique Trunks, Refinish, Repair, Restore*.

They currently live in an 18th century cape cod in Barrington, N.H., where they have converted the 1791 carriage house into a workshop and showroom.

Acknowledgments:

We'd like to thank the following people who helped in making this book possible:

David Edelstein, with whom we began this journey and search almost 30 years ago, we thank for providing invaluable information and for sharing his exquisite trunk collection.

Anne Edelstein Morse for her high level professional photography and image advice.

Armand Poulin for his untiring lugging of trunks up and down stairs to be photographed.

Eve and Colin Williams for making available their extensive collection of trunks.

Eve Edelstein Williams for much needed editorial help.

Rod Morse for his advice and counsel.

Tom Ciccotelli, for generously sharing his collection of early trunk advertising, maker's labels, and shipping labels, as well historical information and advice.

Eric Peterson for endless hours of editing and encouragement.

Churchill Barton for sending us a wide array of advertising, labels, catalogs, and support.

Scott Carlton who contributed a special element to the book.

Nancy Asimakopoulos and Del Priestley for many miles on the road scouting for the best trunks.

Marvin Miller for making available his research into the Saratoga controversy.

Dedication:

This book is dedicated to David Edelstein, brother, mentor, and friend.

Contents

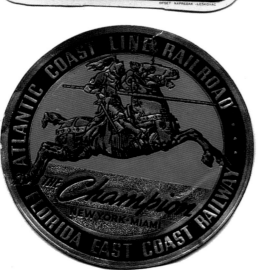

Introduction

Trunks have been around for thousands of years. They've been around trees even longer. Most societies have used trunks, in one form or another since the beginning of history. They were not always referred to as trunks but they still served the same purpose. Chests, boxes, bins, portmanteaus were all essentially trunks by another name.

The materials used for construction were wood, leather, cloth, metal, paper, and wicker. The first trunks were just that: containers made from the hollowed out trunk of a tree or log. Of course, the Egyptians had trunks made from stone but they are more properly called sarcophagi, used in entombment.

Trunks were entirely handmade until the early 19th century and the dawn of the industrial revolution. Bit by bit the several parts of trunks came to be made by machine. Nails evolved from handmade rose head nails to square cut machine-made nails. Likewise, the steel banding was starting to be made by rolling mills rather than hand forged. Lumber for the trunk body was cut in water powered sawmills instead of by hand in a sawpit. Locks, latches, hinges, and all of the other hardware was no longer handmade but stamped, cast, pressed, and otherwise made by newly invented machines.

By the mid 19th century, there was virtually nothing on a trunk that was not made by machine. The trunk itself was still being put together mostly by hand but even that was changing with the coming of nailing machines and presses. As the machines became more efficient and the style of trunks changed, the output increased dramatically.

The last half of the 19th century saw a huge increase in the production of every style of trunk. According to the U.S. Patent Office, in 1860 the total value of trunks produced in the United States was $2,800,000. By 1880, that figure had grown to exceed $7,000,000. Even though machines had taken over a large part of trunk making, the number of people working on trunks more than doubled from about 2,100 to 4,500.

The big makers such as M.M. Secor were producing 80,000 to 100,000 trunks per year at this time. Many of these trunks were shipped to Europe and were brought back to the United States by immigrants. In fact, this double ocean crossing by many thousands of trunks has led to the obscuring of the origins of these trunks. "This trunk was brought over from Europe by my great grandfather," is a statement often heard. Therefore, the trunk was thought to have been made in Europe, when, in fact, it was made in the United States.

Adding further to the confusion over the origin of trunks is the fact that many trunk makers copied each other's styles, often down to the last detail. This was more of a local or regional problem rather than an international one.

The turn of the century saw the introduction of wardrobe style trunks. These huge pieces, with their many drawers and hanger compartment, were designed to act as mini bureaus and closets during long sea passages or on summer trips made to the country by "rusticators." They were often four feet tall or taller and approached 150 to 200 pounds when filled. They needed two strong men or a dolly to move them and were only suitable for transportation on railroads or steamships.

Later, in the early part of the 20th century, trunk styles changed even more. New materials and methods were introduced to make trunks more economical and lighter. Plywood, imitation leather, metal plating, and machine assembly were all added to the trunk equation if not there already.

Then, as transportation changed from railroads and ships to airplanes and automobiles, the era of the trunk slowly came to an end. Hard-bodied suitcases and smaller bags that could easily be carried by one person and stowed in a car trunk or airplane cargo hold replaced the unwieldy trunk as the mode of carrying personal belongings.

By this time, most of the major trunk makers had gone out of business or, if they were inventive like Hartmann, were retooling to produce smaller luggage items.

Some of the better makers, such as Louis Vuitton and Goyard, continued to produce top of the line trunks that were sold to movie stars, moguls, and monarchs who had their own railroads and ships.

This book follows the development of trunks through 150 years. The years 1780 through 1930 were the big years for trunk makers and styles changed from small, plain, handmade trunks to large, fancy, closet-like behemoths. We show the changes, subtle and grand. We list several hundred trunk makers along with some information about where they were located and what they produced. We include a price list for specific trunks and also include a special Valuerator® so that you can determine the value of your own trunk. Also in this book you will find copies of many of the original trunk makers' labels as well as the Victorian prints found in antique trunks.

The M.M. Secor factory turned out 80,000 to 100,000 trunks a year at its peak in the 1880s.

Anatomy of a trunk

Base: The bottom part of the trunk.

Drawbolt: A two-part piece of hardware that tightens the base and lid together with a hook and clamping device (sometimes called latches).

End cap or handle loop: Used to dress up the end of the handle or to actually hold the handle on the trunk.

Handle: Made from leather, brass, or steel. They are fastened to the two ends of the trunk and are used to lift the trunk. On a smaller trunk the handle might be fastened only to the top.

Latch: The latch is a long tongue-shaped piece of metal fastened to the lid that swings down and attaches to the lock plate to secure the trunk.

Lid: The top part of the trunk.

Lip: A 1″ wide strip of steel around the bottom of the lid to help seal the trunk.

Lock plate: Usually attached to the bottom of the trunk. Holds the latch.

Metal trim: Wide strips of flat sheet steel used to dress up and reinforce the trunk, especially along the edges and corners.

Rollers: Metal devices attached to the bottom of the trunk to help it glide across the floor.

Slat: Used to reinforce the trunk, usually made of oak or some other hardwood.

Slat clamp: Holds the slat onto the trunk. These are usually attached to the ends of the slat. They are also attached where one slat meets another.

Stay: A hinged metal device that holds the lid of the trunk up. Many older trunks had cloth stays.

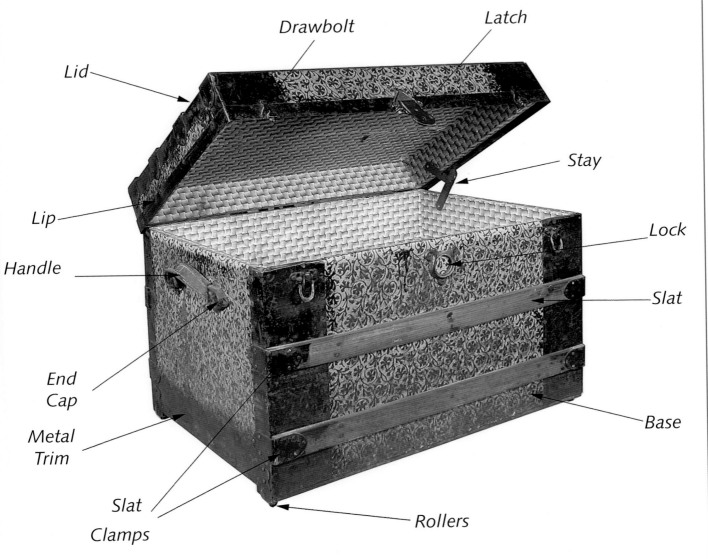

Drawbolt

Latch

Lid

Stay

Lip

Lock

Handle

Slat

End
Cap

Base

Metal
Trim

Slat
Clamps

Rollers

The Saga of the "Saratoga Trunk"

There is some controversy over the definition of a Saratoga Trunk. We have heard a number of descriptions and opinions over the years. Around New England it's not uncommon to hear a fine curved-sided Jenny Lind trunk described as a Saratoga and we referred to them in that way for many years.

A catalog from Seward Trunk and Bag Company of Petersburg, Va., which was sent to us by Marvin Miller, pictures a trunk described as a "Zinc Saratoga. High grade, round top, metal trunk, made attractively and built strong. A very high type of this class of trunk, ornamented with Saddler's nails, high grade trimmings, protected by angle iron and a chain binding. Two Tumbler Excelsior locks. V. & G. fixtures support the tray. Full linen lined, carrying a skirt tray, the tray carrying the S.S. hat crown and lifters." This trunk is, essentially, a fancy dome top trunk.

Miller has researched this subject in exhausting detail and has provided us with many pages and pictures of trunks and articles to bolster his conclusion, that it is only these fancy dome top trunks that describe the Saratoga.

Miller also found an 1898 catalog from the Buffalo Trunk Mfg. Co., including two descriptions. The first, "Saratoga No. 90 - Crystal Covered," pictures a "Full size Barrel Top Box, seventeen slats, top and front slats reversed, iron bottom, heavy corner rollers with clamps and trimmings, including tripod corner clamps on top corners, stitched handles, rollers, patent bolts, brass Victorian malleable scroll binding on top ends, two doors in top, raised hat box in center of tray with shirt compartment on each side, hat box nicely ornamented." The second, "G.P. Saratoga - No. 1," describes a "barrel top box, imitation leather, iron bound, seven long slats, clamped, patent bolts, rollers, set up tray with covered hat box."

A straight-sided Jenny Lind trunk. End view.

Both of these descriptions identify a fancy dome top trunk as a "Saratoga."

It seems that the name Saratoga came from the resort in New York of the same name. Saratoga Springs was a very popular summer destination. It was the premier vacation spot in the country, in its heyday, for the wealthy and influential and many spent the entire season. They brought along enough clothes and other personal goods to last through these lengthy stays. Large containers were needed to carry all of their belongings and the trunk makers complied by styling trunks suited especially for this type of journey. They were large, fancy trunks fitted with many compartments, trays, hangers, and other features.

These top-of-the-line trunks were named "Saratogas" or "Saratoga Grade," or "The Saratoga," and they sold well. The Saratoga Trunk Company, of Saratoga, N.Y., made and sold Saratogas as well, and they were active during the 1860s.

The controversy indicated above is that sometimes a curved-sided Jenny Lind trunk is referred to as a Saratoga. While this may be a correct name for a fancy, compartmented, curved-sided Jenny Lind style trunk, it is not necessarily correct for all curved-sided Jenny Lind trunks.

So herein lies the problem. There are basically two styles of Jenny Lind trunks. The first is curved sided, shaped like an hourglass, and has curves on both the top and the bottom. The second is shaped like a keyhole with straighter lines and more of a tapered bottom rather than curved. They are both Jenny Lind trunks. And when it comes right down to it, you could call either of them a Saratoga if they were especially fancy. But remember to call some of those fancy dome top trunks Saratogas, as well.

See the accompanying pictures for further details.

A curved-sided Jenny Lind trunk. End view.

A Saratoga grade dome top trunk. End view

Saratoga Trunk

Price Guide Introduction

The following price guide covers trunks made from about 1780-1935. If you want to determine the value of any trunk, please refer to the Valuerator System® at the end of the trunk price guide. This system, used in conjunction with the Condition Guide, will help you to figure out what that trunk is worth.

Any price with a "+" after it means that the highest price stated could be increased significantly if the trunk is in mint condition. It wouldn't be unusual for the price to more than double for a pristine condition example.

Trunk prices can vary considerably from region to region and country to country. For example, you would have to spend more money to buy a trunk on the West Coast than in New England. The fact is there are a lot more trunks in the New England area so they are priced accordingly. We have taken that into consideration when writing this book and have tried to achieve a balance.

Another factor that enters into the picture when buying or selling a trunk is the human element. It takes a willing buyer and a willing seller to consummate a deal. Depending on how willing one or the other is will also determine the ultimate price paid.

Flat top, hide-covered stagecoach trunk. This trunk was made of pine and covered with untanned hide with the hair still on. It seems to have been a standard procedure for making trunks during this era from about 1780-1840. The other identifying features of trunks from this era are hand-forged handles, lock, and hinges. Many were adorned with hand-cast brass tacks, as was this example. It also has thin sheet steel reinforcing tabs around the edges of the trunk.

Ca. 1790.

Value: **$200-$600**

End view of the stagecoach trunk showing the hand-forged iron handle.

Early printed canvas-covered, flat top, square trunk. This trunk has an unusual shape with leather trim and brass tacks. The canvas covering is printed in a flower and leaf pattern. The original handles are hand forged. Ca. 1800.
Value: **$200-$400**

David Edelstein

Soft top, leather-covered trunk. This early trunk is entirely handmade and features an unusual soft leather top. It has unique brass tack decoration common to the period, and has hand-forged iron handles, lock, and latch. It has a leather lip to protect from dust, and originally had two additional leather straps that wrapped around the body from back to front. The soft top allows for a laundry compartment accessed through the inside of the lid. When the lid was stuffed with laundry, the top of the trunk was cushioned and doubled as a seat. This is a rare trunk.
Ca. 1810.
Value: **$200-$500**

Antique Trunks

David Edelstein

Side view of hide-covered, round trunk.

Early, hide-covered, round trunk. This unusual
trunk has its original hide covering and hand-
forged handles. Decorated with metal banding
and tacks.
Ca. 1813.
Value: **$700-$1,500**

Leather-covered, flat top, camphor wood trunk. This is a very rare and desirable chest. It is made of
camphor wood with dovetail construction. It was covered with top grain leather and finished with brass
banding on all of the edges and decorated with hundreds of hand-cast brass tacks. The tacks, set in lines
all around the trunk, form an oval on the top and swags on the front. It has a hand-forged lock and
handles. Many of these trunks came from China, but R.H. Hand made this one in Boston. Camphor
wood is fairly common in China and less so in America, although it grows in the South and Southwest.
Camphor wood chests were made in this style for 30 or 40 years from about 1790-1830.
Ca. 1825.
Value: **$1,200-$2,000+**

Curved top, hide-covered trunk. The body is covered with hide, in this case most probably deer hide. It is trimmed with leather and finished with small hand-cast brass tacks. The handles, lock, and latch plate are all hand forged. Notice the scalloped edges of the leather just above the leather lip, and the oval on top created with more brass tacks. Often you will find initials inside these top decorations, probably added at the time of purchase.

Ca.1820.

Value: **$200-$600**

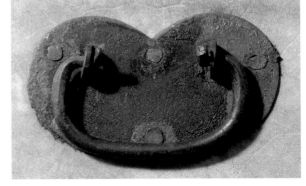

Detail of hand-wrought iron handle and nails.

Detail of leather lip finished with scalloped leather and handmade tacks.

Detail of leather and brass tack oval.

Eve and Colin Williams

Early, leather-covered flat top trunk. This trunk is decorated with scalloped leather trim around the lip, and leather banding attached with brass tacks. There is also an oval on the top of the trunk decorated with leather and brass tacks. The handles are hand wrought and the lock plate is made of steel.
Ca. 1835.
Value: **$200-$450**

Suitcase grouping.
Ca. 1840-1875.

Craig Heindel

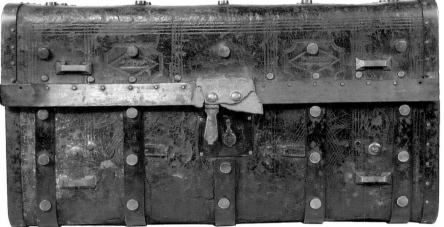

Front view of sole leather trunk. Notice the remnants of a leather lid lift.

Sole leather trunk, made of leather and pressed cardboard. Decorated with steel banding and large brass buttons, the trunk features original lock with brass covering over the keyhole. Originally leather straps wrapped around the body and were guided through brass keepers.
Ca. 1840.
Value: **$250-$500**

Close view of brass buttons and brass keeper.

Detail of hand-tooled leather and large brass buttons.

Canvas-covered oval suitcase. This unusual suitcase features hand-forged hooks and eyes. Decorated with tacks around the edges and seams, this suitcase includes its original handles and medallion. Ca. 1845.
Value: **$145-$325**

Eve and Colin Williams

Pre Civil War Era leather-covered hand trunk. This trunk includes brass tacks and top mounted brass handle. Original leather trim around the lid, and original lock mechanism.
Ca. 1845.
Value: **$125-$250**

Three leather-covered hand trunks, all diminutive, with their leather handles on top. These small trunks display most of the features found on their larger counterparts: tooled leather, hand-cast brass tacks, and leather lip on the two smaller ones. The leather lip that hangs down from the lid protects the interior from dust and dirt filtering in. Note the largest of the three has a metal band around the lip, an indication of a later trunk.
Ca. 1850-1860.
Value: **$150-$350**

Eve and Colin Williams

Three Civil War Era trunks. The smallest features all of the components found on a high quality trunk of its day: brass buttons, leather straps and buckles, iron banding, and original large leather flap to protect the lock from weather. The middle trunk is paper covered, tooled to resemble leather, and also features the metal banding, brass buttons, leather straps and buckles on the front, and a small leather lid lifter. In addition, this trunk has hardwood slats across the top, not present on the other two. This indicates a later trunk. The largest, black leather covered, is also decorated with brass buttons, has a fifth iron strap across the top, a large leather flap over the lock, and leather straps and buckles on the front.
Ca. 1850-1860.
Value: **$250-$800**

Eve and Colin Williams

Group of doll trunks.
Ca. 1850-1920

Eve and Colin Williams

Leather-covered, flat top pre-Civil War Era trunk. This trunk features leather covering, metal front-to-back banding with large brass buttons, and the original leather lock flap. It also features the extra leather straps and buckles for extra security.
Ca. 1850.
Value: **$300-$700**

Eve and Colin Williams

Curved-top, brass bound, embossed leather trunk. This is an outstanding trunk of the era. It has brass clad steel straps, a fancy brass lock, sculpted leather handles, and a sculpted leather lifter. It also has an interior tray, and the many large brass buttons round it out nicely. It was so highly prized by its owner that a custom canvas cover was made for it, to add protection during travel.
Ca. 1850.
Value: **$1,100-$1,600**

Detail of brass-bound trunk fitted with custom-made canvas covering.

This suitcase is made of pine and covered with leather. It also features large brass buttons and a hand-forged lock. It contains a lidded interior compartment, as did many of the suitcases from this era. The angled top and bottom of this suitcase are in the Jenny Lind style. The exterior is covered with tooled leather and has large eagles embossed on both sides.

Ca. 1850.

Value: **$300-$600**

The cloth-lined, compartmented interior of the Jenny Lind suitcase.

View of Jenny Lind suitcase, illustrating shape, metal banding, and embossed leather covering.

Eve and Colin Williams

Leather-covered, flat top pre-Civil War trunk. This is a great example of an early and finely made trunk. With embossed brown leather covering, it has many large brass buttons and a fancy brass lock. It also displays five metal bands around the body compared to the customary four. The trunk is enhanced with details including the sculpted handles and an interior tray. The outstanding condition of this trunk increases its value substantially.
Ca. 1850.
Value: **$900-$1,500**

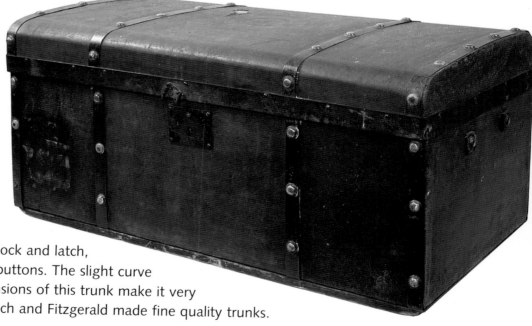

Slightly curved top, leather-covered pre-Civil War trunk. This trunk was made by Crouch and Fitzgerald, and is likely one of their very first efforts. It has a finely embossed leather covering, steel banding, lock and latch, and features large brass buttons. The slight curve of the top and the dimensions of this trunk make it very pleasing to the eye. Crouch and Fitzgerald made fine quality trunks.
Ca. 1850.
Value: **$550-$800**

Antique Trunks

Black leather covered, low profile pre-Civil War trunk. Reinforced with steel bands and decorated with handmade brass buttons, this is a wonderful example in almost original condition. Note the use of leather for the lip and the absence of wooden slats, both indications of an early trunk. The lock, hasp, and plate are made of steel with a brass keyhole cover and trim. Ca.1850.

Value: **$400-$700**

Closer view of the lock shows fine craftsmanship.

End view of pre-Civil War trunk showing early treatment of handles.

Brass bound, curved-sided Jenny Lind trunk. This is one of the most sought after trunks of the period. It is a Jenny Lind with an additional curve in both the bottom and the lid, and it is banded with brass-clad steel straps. The banding is decorated with small handmade copper buttons and the wooden slats are made of a hardwood. The lock and a fancy brass lock plate are not unusual on a trunk of this quality. Missing are two leather strap and buckle assemblies that came down from the lid and attached to the front of the trunk. Because it is considered more esthetically pleasing, the curved-sided Jenny Lind is much more desirable than the straight-sided model, and could also be called a Saratoga. Ca. 1855.
Value: **$1,200-$1,600+**

Detail of fancy brass lock plate.

Side view of curved-sided Jenny Lind showing original handle and hand wrought hardware and brass buttons.

Canvas-covered Jenny Lind-style trunk. This graceful trunk has front-to-back brass banding with buttons and its original brass lock plate. These types of trunks were named after the Swedish singer of the same name and made for about a 20-year period from 1850-1870. Jenny Lind came to America for a tour in the mid 1850s and carried a trunk of this style with her. It's up for debate whether she brought the trunk with her from Europe or purchased it after she arrived in the United States. Regardless, she was very popular and her distinctive trunk became all the rage. Some of these trunks were very plain with little or no brass hardware, while others were adorned with brass straps, fancy brass locks, and large brass buttons.
Ca. 1855.
Value: **$600-$1,500+**

Eve and Colin Williams

The interior of the embossed leather Jenny Lind-style suitcase, showing the original paper lining and lidded compartment.

Leather-covered, brass and iron trimmed suitcase.
The leather covering of this suitcase is decorated with a striking embossed medallion pattern on the sides. The steel banding on its edges is decorated with brass buttons. Larger brass buttons accentuate the embossing on the sides. On the inside, there is a compartment with door. The canted top and bottom of this suitcase are in the Jenny Lind style.
Ca. 1855.
Value: **$400-$600**

Black leather-covered suitcase. This suitcase has an embossed leather covering and leather handles. The leather is stitched right into the wooden body of the suitcase.
Ca. 1855.
Value: **$250-$350**

Paper-covered Jenny Lind doll trunk. It is extremely rare to find a trunk like this. It has a pine body covered with paper that has been printed to look like embossed leather. It comes with an interior tray, wrought iron lock, and stamped steel handle end caps. A nice detail is the leather dust seal around the top lip.
Ca. 1855.
Value: **$350-$600+**

Jenny Lind doll trunk, showing papered interior, and tray.

Canvas-covered
Louis Vuitton steamer trunk.
This trunk's canvas covering is painted in the
Vuitton "Trianon" pattern. The trunk has horizontal
hardwood slats with brass buttons, and original hardware and lock,
each embossed with the distinctive "LV" monogram.
Ca. 1854.
Value: **$1,200-$2,500**

David Edelstein

Eve and Colin Williams

Brass bound,
leather-covered,
straight-sided Jenny Lind
doll trunk. This is an exquisite
example of the Jenny Lind trunk, in miniature. It has an embossed black leather covering, brass
buttons, and brass straps. It also has a fitted lid compartment and interior tray. Instead of handles, it
has little brass rings on the ends. This is a rare find in such excellent condition. Two other nice details
are the brass plate surrounding the keyhole and the small leather lid lifter.
Ca. 1860.
Value: **$500-$800**

This miniature, curved-sided Jenny Lind trunk is one of the very nicest, top quality in its day, and in extremely good original condition today. This doll-sized trunk boasts all of the appropriate accoutrements of its full-sized counterparts. The leather trim, banding, handles, and lift are handsomely attached with handmade brass buttons. The keyhole is surrounded with brass and the paper covering though slightly worn, is still exceptional.
Ca. 1855.
Value: **$800-$1,200**

Eve and Colin Williams

End view of curved-sided Jenny Lind doll trunk. Notice the beautifully proportioned shape, and 150-year-old paper covering.

Leather-covered suitcase. This is a well-made, red leather-covered suitcase with a compartment in the interior. It has a wrought iron lock and small brass buttons to protect it when open. Early suitcases are somewhat rare to find because they were well used and very often thrown away.
Ca. 1855.
Value: **$200-$350**

Eve and Colin Williams

Antique Trunks

David Edelstein

Round-sided Jenny Lind style trunk. This high-style trunk is leather covered and has hardwood slats attached with metal clamps decorated with brass buttons. The front-to-back metal banding is also enhanced with brass buttons. The lock mechanism and brass oval around the keyhole are original. When it was made, this trunk also had leather straps that wrapped around the body and buckled in the front. Ca. 1860.

Value: **$600-$1,500**

Leather-covered, flat top Civil War Era trunk. Featuring front-to-back metal banding with brass buttons, this trunk also has its original leather lift and lock. Originally two leather straps came down from the lid and buckled on the front.

Ca. 1860.

Value: **$300-$650**

Zinc-covered, curved-sided
Jenny Lind trunk. Extremely rare and possibly
unique, this Jenny Lind is perfectly proportioned in height, width, and shape.
It is the only metal-covered Jenny Lind that we have come across. There is a fitted compartment in
the lid and a hinged tray that is collapsible and can be folded and put in the bottom of the trunk. It
has oak slats, iron banding, and large, flat brass buttons. The lock and latch are brass. Perhaps this
trunk was custom-made for a ship's captain, the zinc covering giving extra protection from the weather
and the sea.
Ca. 1860.
Value: **$2,500-$3,500**

End view of beautifully curved, zinc clad Jenny Lind trunk.
Notice the cast iron handle caps. Hand-wrought iron
brackets coming up from the bottom and attention to detail
indicate craftsmanship of the highest quality.

Detail of the horizontal slat attachment.

Detail of brass lock mechanism.

Canvas-covered, Jenny Lind-style brass-bound trunk. This trunk has brass clad banding and brass buttons, hardwood slats nicely tapered on the ends, and a brass lock and plate with lockable brass keyhole cover. The leather straps and buckles, and the leather lift, are original. Notice the combining of metals, with the black steel lip used in conjunction with the brass.

Ca. 1860.

Value: **$1,200-$1,800+**

End view of canvas-covered Jenny Lind trunk.

End view of a curved-sided Jenny Lind trunk.

Leather-covered pine body suitcase, Jenny Lind style. This suitcase has steel banding on the edges trimmed with brass buttons. The handles and straps are leather, and the interior is divided into two lined compartments.
Ca. 1860.
Value: **$375-$475**

Repaired, refinished, and restored flat top Civil War Era trunk. The body is pine, and the strapping and lip are made of steel. Handmade brass buttons decorate the banding, and the lock is original.
Ca.1860.
Value: **$600-$700**

Civil War Era trunk with brass buttons, in the process of being refinished.

Flat top, paper-covered Civil War Era trunk.
The paper covering is printed to resemble tooled leather, and notice
that the "steel bands" usually seen on this style of trunk are, in this case, printed too. It has original steel
banding around the lip, and original lock plate and latch.
Ca. 1864.
Value: **$300-$500**

Curved top, paper-covered Civil War Era trunk. This is another example of the trunks made during this era using paper that was printed to look like embossed leather. This was a very inexpensive way to finish off a trunk during this period of leather shortage. This one actually has the design patent date 1864 printed on the front top. This is a plainer example of the style, with no brass, copper, or other fancy adornments. These solid trunks were produced in abundance during a very short time span of about four or five years. Although these trunks were not very weather resistant, many of them survive due to the sheer numbers produced. This is the start of the era of trunks made entirely of machine-produced parts. Everything on this type of trunk, including the wood, lock, other hardware, covering, and nails, were made by machine. The trunk was then assembled by hand.
Ca. 1864.
Value: **$150-$250**

Printed paper-covered Civil War Era trunk. This trunk has metal front-to-back banding with brass buttons, as well as rare faux leather embossing. Addition of the wooden slats on top of the lid is indicative of the period. Leather straps with buckles and the leather lid lift are nice details. The original lock and latch are intact.
Ca. 1864.
Value: **$250-$600**

Curved top, leather-covered Civil War Era trunk. Trunks were beginning to acquire a more elegant look by this time. This curved top trunk has a very pleasing shape and style. It has little adornment, but what it does have is subtly pleasing. Embossed brown leather, oak slats, and iron banding with small copper buttons add to the stately appearance of this trunk. Ca. 1865.
Value: **$150-$500**

Canvas-covered, flat top Civil War Era trunk. The straightforward construction and design of this trunk give it a solid, respectable look. The body is pine and the banding is made of steel, as are the latch and lock plate. The wooden slats across the top are hardwood. Originally this trunk also featured two leather buckles, one on either side of the lock. An excellent example of a trunk from this era, these canvas-covered trunks were made from about 1860-1870, and were put together by hand from machine-made parts. They sometimes had brass locks and fancy brass buttons of various sizes.
Ca. 1865.
Value: **$175-$325**

Bed trunk.
Flat top, embossed leather-covered
Civil War Era trunk. This is a most unusual and rare trunk
in that it opens from one end and makes into a bed, and has two
compartments in the interior fashioned to hold the mattress and
bedding. The exterior utilizes the metal banding of the period, with the
lock on the end, and iron handles. Additionally, three leather straps
with buckles wrapped around the trunk providing extra security. This
trunk was made by Summers of St. Louis, Mo., and has its stamp on
the head piece.
Ca. 1865.
Value: **$3,500-$4,500**

Detail of manufacturer's patent label.

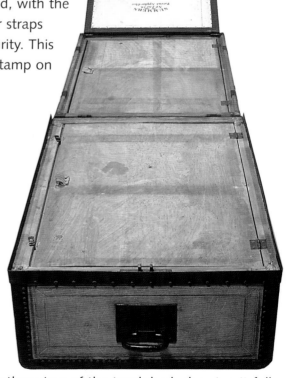

Another view of the trunk bed, showing it fully
extended. Notice the mahogany framed head
piece with a soft canvas insert that folds out.
Total length of the bed is six feet.

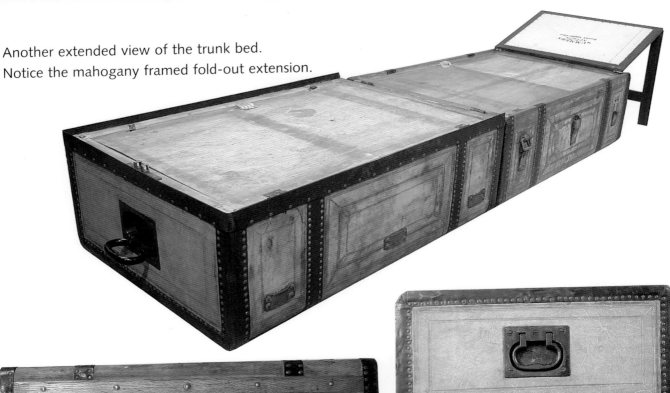

Another extended view of the trunk bed.
Notice the mahogany framed fold-out extension.

Top view showing metal banding and tooled
leather covering.

End view of trunk bed showing recessed
handle, side lock with key, and metal edging.

Detail of side lock with key.

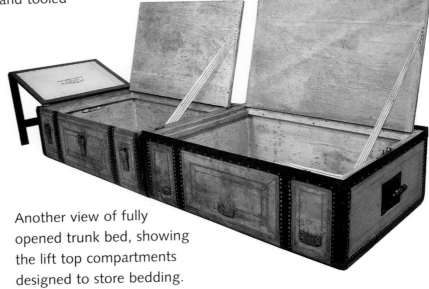

Another view of fully
opened trunk bed, showing
the lift top compartments
designed to store bedding.

Leather-covered, flat top Civil War Era trunk. This flat top trunk has its original leather covering, handles, and lock flap as well its original steel banding with brass buttons.
Ca. 1865.
Value: **$250-$700**

Eve and Colin Williams

Black leather-covered hand trunk, with iron lip band, and brass lock and latch plate. The leather is subtly tooled and the leather handle mounted on top.
Ca. 1867.
Value: **$125-$250**

Detail of the brass bound trunk.

Brass bound, curved top Civil War Era trunk.
This trunk has a pebbled coating of coal tar over the leather covering as an added weatherproofing.
It also has copper buttons and a brass lock. This is the start of the golden era of trunks, when the tops were rounded and a small amount of brass ornamentation added greatly to the esthetic value of trunks. The brass strapping is actually paper-thin rolled brass wrapped around the steel banding.
It's rare to find a trunk with this coal tar coating and brass banding in good condition.
Ca. 1865.
Value: **$500-$1,800+**

Curved top, canvas-covered Civil War Era trunk with brass banding. This trunk has the nicely formed curved top that is so desirable. It also has hardwood slats, brass banding, copper buttons, and a very unusual brass lock with a cast brass dolphin keyhole cover. All of this adds up to make this a very rare and desirable trunk. This also could be considered a transitional trunk style made for less than 10 years. Noted for its sophisticated shape and the addition of a gently curving top, this trunk style announces the start of the golden era of trunks. Trunks of this type were covered with black leather, black canvas, or pebbled leather. Pebbled leather is leather that has had a slathering of tar applied as an additional weather-proofing, giving the trunk a rough textured surface.
Ca. 1865.
Value: **$500-$1,800+**

Interior view of the dolphin trunk.

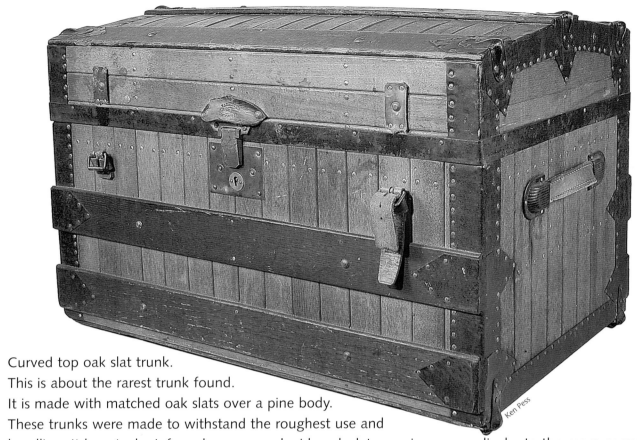

Curved top oak slat trunk.

This is about the rarest trunk found.

It is made with matched oak slats over a pine body.

These trunks were made to withstand the roughest use and handling. It has steel reinforced corners and wide oak slats running perpendicular to the more narrow oak slats of the body. It also has cast iron wraparound rollers on the bottom and cast iron handle end caps. It came with a brass lock, fitted tray, and compartments in the lid. These oak slat trunks were made by Excelsior Trunk Company of Philadelphia, Pa.

Ca. 1870.

Value: **$800-$2,500+**

The brass lock of the oak slat trunk showing the patent date 1870.

The cast iron handle end caps of the oak slat trunk.

The Excelsior oak slat trunk showing an end view.

The lid lifter of the oak slat trunk showing the name Excelsior.

Early, leather-covered, bevel top steamer trunk. This distinctive bevel top trunk features steel edging cut in a scalloped pattern and attached with nails. The trunk includes horizontal hardwood slats attached with brass clamps and domed brass buttons. The leather covering is embossed and the fancy brass lock mechanism is original. Extremely rare. Ca. 1870.
Value: **$500-$2,200**

Early, high-end, dome top doll trunk. This doll trunk has horizontal hardwood slats with brass clamps on the dome top. It includes steel trim and lid banding. The fancy brass lock mechanism is original. This trunk was covered with embossed leather. This example looks pretty rough, but it's still a rare find and will be a good candidate for refinishing. Ca. 1870.
Value: **$250-$900**

Low profile, flat top steamer trunk.
A nice example of what high quality materials and
craftsmanship can produce. This is an early trunk of this style. The body is made of pine, with oak slats, a brass lock, and forged steel handles, not often used by American trunk makers. Because of its small size, it came with a handle on the front so that it could also be carried like a suitcase. It also has leather edging held on with many brass tacks. This is really a transitional steamer of a type that was made for only a few years from about 1850-1870, from a combination of handmade and machined materials. The locks were often hand forged while the lumber was cut in a sawmill. The canvas covering was made in a factory as well. The whole trunk was put together by hand with these assembled materials.
Ca. 1870.
Value: **$250-$400+**

Dome top, paper-covered doll trunk. The paper covering, made to resemble an alligator embossed metal clad trunk, is very unusual. The style is clearly that of an early dome top steamer. The embossed metal-covered trunks that it emulates didn't arrive on the scene until the 1870s, but the paper covering would have been common to the Civil War Era. This wonderful little trunk gives us a glimpse of the transition between two styles.
Ca. 1870.
Value: **$125-$400**

Eve and Colin Williams

Early, leather-covered, dome top steamer trunk. This early steamer features fluted hardwood horizontal slats with decorative steel clamps. It includes leather covering with steel covering on the sides and front. The lock mechanism is original.
Ca. 1870.
Value: **$300-$900**

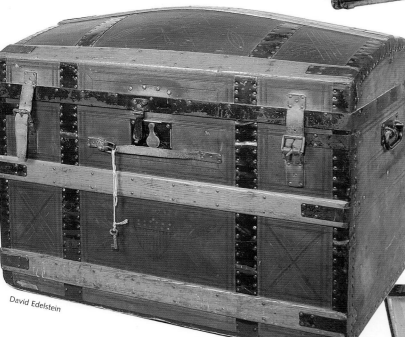

David Edelstein

Early, leather-covered, dome top steamer trunk. This Crouch & Fitzgerald trunk has horizontal hardwood slats and front-to-back metal banding. The leather covering is decoratively embossed. The lock mechanism is original and includes the key.
Ca. 1870.
Value: **$600-$1,500**

Open lid view showing the curve top tray and compartment.

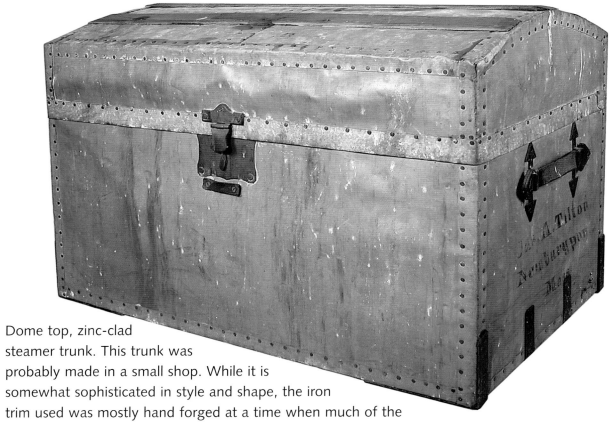

Dome top, zinc-clad steamer trunk. This trunk was probably made in a small shop. While it is somewhat sophisticated in style and shape, the iron trim used was mostly hand forged at a time when much of the same materials were being produced by machines. The walls of the trunk are doubled, with an air space of about one half inch in between, and the whole body of the trunk is covered with a layer of thin zinc applied with copper tacks. It has a compartment in the lid, brass lock, and a sliding half tray. It also has very heavy hand-forged corners on the bottom and hand-forged handle loops.
Ca. 1870.
Value: **$600-$1,600**

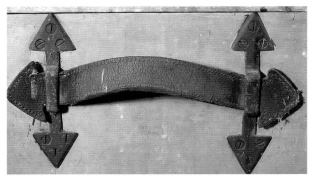

Detail showing the large, heavy-duty, hand-forged handle loops.

Interior view of the zinc-clad trunk.

Embossed metal wall trunk, with an almost flat top. This metal clad trunk is embossed with flowers, vines, and the alligator pattern; somewhat unusual to find multi patterns on one trunk. This is a well made trunk with decorative slat clamps, a metal lid lifter and particularly nice dimensions, making it a step above the average. It is a wall trunk made by Miller. Notice the detail and operation of the patented hinge, which allows the trunk to be placed directly against the wall and still be opened. Ca. 1890.

Value: **$800-$1,200**

Detail showing the patented hinge of the Miller wall trunk.

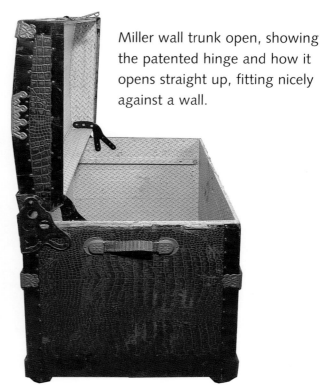

Miller wall trunk open, showing the patented hinge and how it opens straight up, fitting nicely against a wall.

Flat top, canvas-covered,
small-sized steamer trunk made
by Louis Vuitton. This trunk has a brass lock,
walnut slats, brass buttons, and wrought iron handles.
This striped pattern was made by Vuitton for a few short years
from about 1872-1888 and is very desirable among collectors. It has the original label inside that
looks like the trunk itself and the signature criss-cross ribbon in the lid. Notice, also, the way the stays
are attached in such a way as to disappear inside the edge of the trunk when closed. Vuitton trunks
were well marked and this one is no exception. Along with the Vuitton name on the label, it also has
the initials LV stamped on the handles, and the whole name and address stenciled on the bottom.
Later LV trunks had the company's name monogrammed on the canvas and also had the whole name
stamped on every brass button.
Ca. 1875.
Value: **$1,500-$2,500**

Front view of the Louis Vuitton trunk

End view of the Louis Vuitton trunk.

Antique Trunks

Inside of the lid showing the criss-cross ribbon pattern seen in most Louis Vuitton trunks.

Inside view showing the disappearing stay.

End view showing the iron handle with Louis Vuitton monogram.

Bottom of the trunk showing the stenciled Louis Vuitton information.

Metal-covered,
dome top steamer trunk.
This graceful trunk has
horizontal hardwood slats,
metal trim, and its original lock
and latches. This is a fine example of the most sturdy of
trunks, designed to hold up to rough handling.
Ca. 1870.
Value: **$200-$400**

End view, showing metal edge
covering and steel lip banding.

Front view showing graceful curve of dome and
latches.

Detail of
embossed
iron handle
cap.

Detail of
decorative
cast iron
corner.

Embossed metal-covered, curved top trunk. This wood trunk features horizontal hardwood slats with cast iron latches, lovely leaf and vine embossing, and original leather handles. The lock is also original.
Ca. 1870.
Value: **$250-$650**

Leather-covered dome top steamer trunk. High-quality workmanship and materials are the earmarks of this early dome top. The slat clamps are bulbous and heavy; the handle end caps are cast iron, as are the latches. It is covered with hand-embossed leather and has a high-quality lock and latch with a leather lock cover/lid lifter. This trunk was made using 10 oak slats and it also has wrap-around rollers on the bottom. It also came with a tray and compartments in the lid. This style marked the next step in trunk evolution, with the elegant rise of its high dome top set against the square shape of the main body that give it a look of sophistication and beauty. Trunks from this period often had fancy brass locks, and one or two colorful Victorian prints on the inside. These remain the most popular trunks today.
Ca. 1870.
Value: **$300-$650**

End view of leather-covered dome top steamer, showing original leather handle, metal edging with bulbous slat clamps, and molded casters.

Metal-covered, dome top steamer trunk. This is an example of a medium quality early dome top. It has smooth metal covering the pine body, somewhat plain slat clamps, and a low rise to the dome. It is equipped with two locks, which give it a little bit of a lift, as do the fluted oak slats, which are nicely arranged. Ca. 1875.
Value: **$200-$400**

Embossed metal-covered, dome top steamer trunk, featuring an alligator pattern. The hardwood slats go from front to back on the top, and up and down on the front. This is a type of trunk that was made by the larger makers such as Secor and Duluth. Also, note the double lock on the front and the fancy slat clamps. Ca. 1875.
Value: **$200-$500**

Leather-covered suitcase. This suitcase may be of English origin. It contains a red velvet covered interior and tooled leather exterior, with the leather stitched directly into the wood. It has small brass buttons along the center strip and larger brass buttons securing the leather handles; very fine quality. Ca. 1875.
Value: **$250-$500**

Eve and Colin Williams

Dome top, zinc-covered steamer. This is an early example of this type of dome top trunk. It has herringbone embossed zinc covering the whole trunk and scalloped sheet steel trim along the corners. It also features oak slats that were steamed and formed in a mold to fit over the top. Included on this trunk are cast iron wraparound rollers, cast iron side flip latches, and a fancy brass lock. The solid zinc and zinc-plated trunks were seldom painted, and resulted in a trunk with a very bold character, such as this zinc-plated one. The silver color of the zinc plays off against the black trim and oak slats, really bringing this dome top to the apex of the trunk maker's art. Ca. 1879.
Value: **$700-$1,100**

Dome top embossed metal steamer. Embossed metal trunks can be quite nice. Some were painted while others were zinc plated or even solid zinc. This trunk displays one of the many geometric patterns used. It has slat clamps on top that aren't really fancy, but they do have petal-like shapes on the ends and a bulbous middle. The bottom clamps are plainer but also have the bulbous centers. The latches are cast and the lock is typical of trunks made during this era. The handle end caps are cast iron and embossed with anchors, and the top oak slats are fluted. Ca. 1880.
Value: **$250-$600**

Embossed metal-covered dome top steamer trunk. A solid, well built trunk. Not a very fancy trunk, except in the floral embossed metal and the extraordinary embossed lock. It has cast iron latches and interior compartments. It also has wraparound rollers on the bottom. The wide, plain metal trim on each end detracts somewhat from the beauty of this trunk and gives it a look of heaviness. However, its dome top and wide oak slats make it a desirable trunk. Embossed metal was first used in the early 1870s and continued through the turn of the century. The patterns were many and varied including stars, leaf and vine, spirals, herringbone, basket weave, and more. This covering is usually found on curved top or dome top trunks. Flat top trunks were made with this covering but not many survived. The pattern was often painted in two tones, with the background one color and the raised embossing another. Look for strong colors and metal in good condition.
Ca. 1880.
Value: **$200-$500**

Antique Trunks

Early, canvas-covered wardrobe trunk. This trunk has original metal edging, latches, and lock.
Ca. 1880.
Value: **$600-$1,200**

Interior view of wardrobe.
Note wood hanger and drawers
with original leather pulls.

Detail of latch.

Detail of stamped metal label on the outside.

Detail of original leather handle.

Eve and Colin Williams

Repaired and refinished curved top steamer trunk.
The body is pine and the slats are oak. The hardware is all original,
including the working lock. The cast iron lid lift has nice detail, as do the oversized latches.
Large steel headed tacks both attach and decorate the slats.
Ca. 1880.
Value: **$700-$800**

Heavily reinforced leather-
covered theatrical trunk.
This trunk has front-to-
back metal banding, many
tacks, as well as metal
edge and corner pieces.
Trunks used in the theater
were not only heavy duty,
but also extra strong. They
were often moved daily
from city to city and had to
withstand the hardest of use.
Ca. 1883.
Value: **$600-$1,200**

Detail of front reinforcement and latch.

View showing original leather handle and cast metal reinforcements. Note printed crown and "Melansons" labeling.

Detail of theatrical troupe sign painted on the trunk.

Curved top, embossed metal half trunk. One of the most exquisite of trunks is the half trunk. Sometimes called a hat trunk, these little wonders have a style that is filled with grace. They have all of the materials and hardware of their larger kin, but on a much smaller scale. This one has a metal covering that was embossed to look like canvas. It has cast iron handle end caps and rosettes on the front. Ca. 1885.
Value: **$250-$600**

Canvas-covered, dome top steamer trunk. This is a typical trunk of the period with a shape and style used by many makers. It's plain and simple but with heavy-duty latches, a brass lock, and cast rollers on the bottom. It also has a metal lid lifter. Most trunks of this type had a tray in the bottom section and compartments in the lid. If these components are still intact add 10 percent to the value. Ca. 1885.
Value: **$250-$400**

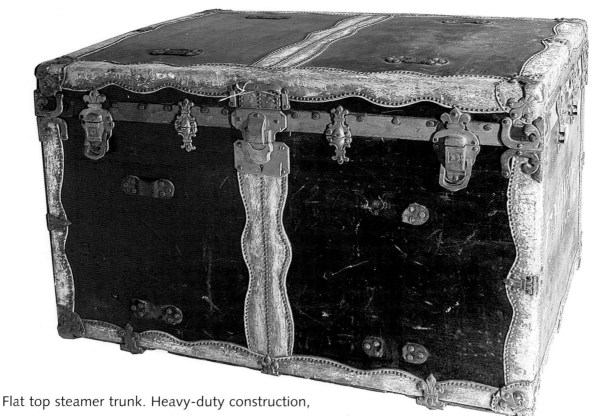

Flat top steamer trunk. Heavy-duty construction,
pig skin trim, cast iron hardware, and a strong lock make this a trunk
that can go through the roughest handling with ease. Made by Drucker in the late 19th century,
the body is either pine or plywood and covered with leather.
Ca. 1885.
Value: **$200-$300**

European dome top
steamer trunk. This
metal-covered trunk
is decorated all over
with little tacks,
giving it an unusual
quilted look. Metal
handles, not found
on trunks made in
America after the
early 1800s, are
typical of European
trunks, as is this
type of lock.
Ca. 1885.
Value: **$125-$300**

Eve and Colin Williams

Flat top, metal-covered
steamer trunk. This is a most
unusual trunk in its construction. Notice how
the top has gently curving corners on the front and back.
The oak slats were softened in a steam cabinet and bent in a mold to fit the curves. The whole
trunk is covered with painted sheet steel, with steel lock and latches as well as steel lifter above the
lock. The trunk's fancy embossed slat clamps, three fingered clamps on the edges, and medallions
on front provide a nice counterpoint to the simplicity of the design. The interior is nicely fitted with
lidded tray, hatbox, top compartment, and four Victorian prints.
Ca. 1885.
Value: **$700-$900**

This view shows the fancy fitted interior
of the trunk. It has a compartment in
the lid that is secured with a door and
two compartments in the tray, one of
which is a hat box. It is also adorned
with several colorful Victorian prints, a
common practice during this period.

Curved top, canvas-covered European steamer. The top of this trunk has a nice pleasing curve, and is accented by thin hardwood slats and large brass buttons. It has two steel locks and wrought iron handles. It is covered with a coarse painted canvas seldom seen on American trunks.
Ca. 1885.
Value: **$300-$500**

David Johns

Repaired, restored, and refinished steamer trunk. The edges are trimmed with tin, the slats of a hardwood, and all hardware is original. The latches feature built in lifts, and the original lock is in working order.
Ca.1885.
Value: **$600-$700**

Detail of lock and plate.

Metal-covered, curved top European steamer. Typical of the European trunks of this period, this trunk has angles that are a bit sharper than its American counterparts. It has fluted hardwood slats, steel latches and lock, as well as the distinctive wrought iron handles. The sheet metal covering the major body of the trunk is zinc plated and the metal trim on the corners is brass plated.
Ca. 1890.
Value: **$175-$325**

Detail of iron handle.

Flat top steamer trunk with rounded edges front and back, canvas covered with oak slats and leather trim. Brass plated hardware and lock with wraparound leather straps that buckled on the front were also original to this trunk. Note the extra set of drawbolts or latches on the front. These insured that the trunk closed with extra security.
Ca. 1890.
Value: **$200-$600**

Eve and Colin Williams

Canvas-covered dresser trunk.
This unusual front opening dresser trunk has
horizontal hardwood slats as well as front-to-back and
side-to-side metal banding.
Ca. 1890.
Value: **$250-$1,200+**

Open view showing
inset mirror with decora-
tion and drawers.

David Edelstein

Early, canvas-covered,
flat top Louis Vuitton steamer trunk.
This trunk has horizontal hardwood slats
attached with brass buttons and clamps. The canvas
covering is printed in a Damier pattern used by Louis Vuitton
for only eight years (1888-1896). It includes all brass locks and handles
with leather trim. Brass buttons are embossed with "Louis Vuitton."
Ca. 1888.
Value: **$2,500-$4,500**

Detail of Louis Vuitton brass handle with trademark embossed into the handle
plate and each brass button individually.

Detail of Louis Vuitton brass latch, embossed with L.V., the individually embossed brass tacks, and the design of the canvas covering.

Detail of barrel-shaped caster.

Interior view showing the hallmark Vuitton quilted lid.

Flat top steamer trunk with hardwood slats, steel hardware, and leather straps with buckles around the body. The latches feature built in lid lifts, and the lock and plate are brass. The guides on either side of the lock are made of steel, and the edging and banding are leatherette.

Ca. 1892.

Value: **$150-$300**

Detail of brass lock, Pat. 1892.

Another view showing off the heavy-duty slat clamps and corners. The addition of the guides tended to keep a trunk straight and true to shape, and this trunk is a good example of that.

Detail of latch with built in lift, guide, and original buckle and leather strap.

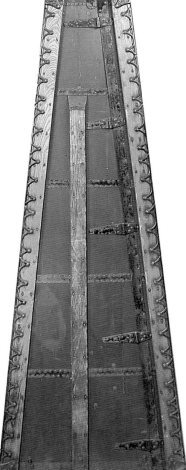

A wonderful example of a specialty trunk: a canvas-covered, steamer style harp case, approximately 6 feet tall. There were not very many of these made. Taylor, a maker of high-quality, heavy-duty trunks, made this particular one. Notice the many cast iron finger reinforcements along the edges. This is also a feature found on their smaller trunks. All of the latches are also cast iron. Made for heavy-duty use. Ca. 1895.
Value: **$2,500-$3,500**

HANDLE WITH CARE.

VALUABLE INSTRUMENT.

Harp case standing on its end.

Detail of cast iron finger reinforcements.

Detail of corner reinforcement on Taylor harp case.

A view of the fancy cast iron latch.

Closer view of fancy brass lock mechanism embossed with Taylor's trademark.

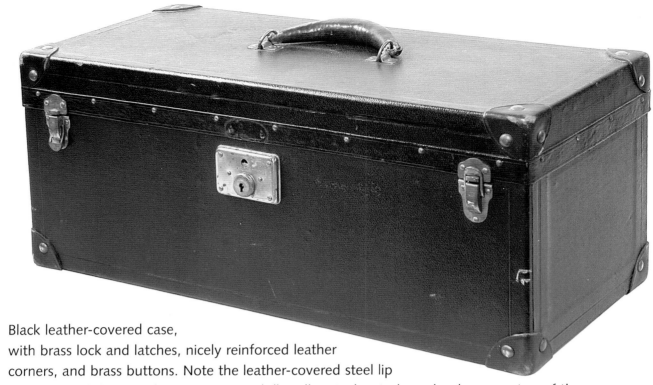

Black leather-covered case,
with brass lock and latches, nicely reinforced leather
corners, and brass buttons. Note the leather-covered steel lip
attached with brass tacks. A suitcase style handle attaches to brass hardware on top of the case.
A traveling salesman most probably used this case, judging by the quilted interior. He would have
carried such a case, containing samples of his merchandise, from place to place.
Ca. 1895.
Value: **$150-$300**

Doll trunk featuring
crystallized metal finish.
A fairly rare finish to find
in good condition, most
often the finish is badly
scratched or rubbed off.
They were often covered
with shellac, which
yellows over the years.
Best thing to do with
these trunks is to leave
them alone. If you try
working on the finish, it
will usually deteriorate
further.
Ca. 1895.
Value: **$125-$250**

Flat top steamer trunk with pine body covered with canvas, and trimmed with hardwood slats. The corner metal and the front-to-back metal straps are made of tin, with the lip and hardware of steel. The brass plated lock, iron finger clamp above the lock, and the addition of the guides on either side of the lock, are all indications of a well-made trunk.
Ca. 1895.
Value: **$100-$350**

Detail of latch. Note the built in lift in the top section.

Detail of guide, an addition that made for a more secure fit of the lid, preventing undue stress on the hinges.

Detail of brass-plated lock common to this period.

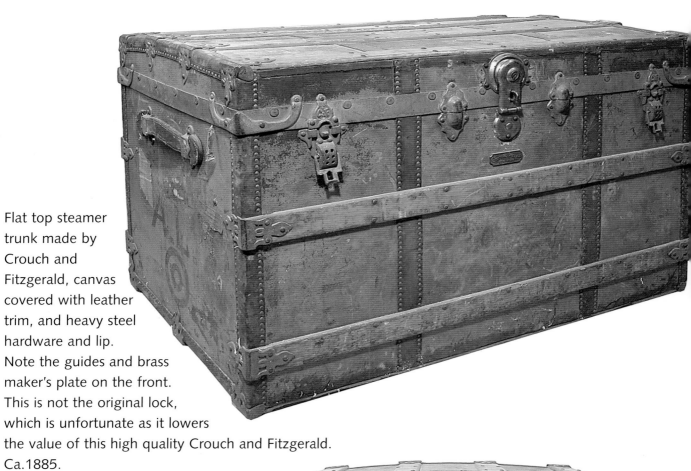

Flat top steamer trunk made by Crouch and Fitzgerald, canvas covered with leather trim, and heavy steel hardware and lip. Note the guides and brass maker's plate on the front. This is not the original lock, which is unfortunate as it lowers the value of this high quality Crouch and Fitzgerald. Ca.1885.
Value: **$200-$400**

End view of Crouch and Fitzgerald steamer trunk. Note the beautiful and heavy-duty clamps, and reinforcement at the corners of the lip.

Heavy-duty iron clamp attaching hardwood slat to body of trunk.

Detail of latch and corner hardware. Notice the C&F embossed into the metal.

Detail showing anchor-style handles and embossed heavyweight handle caps.

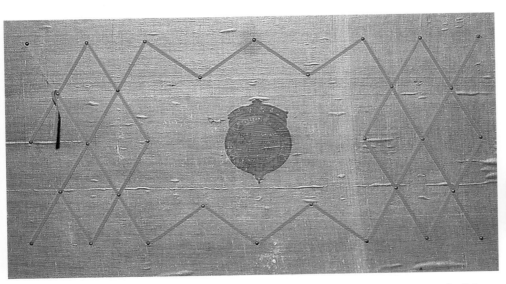

Detail of lid interior with Crouch and Fitzgerald label in center, and ribbon design much like that seen in Louie Vuitton trunks.

Detail of nicely engineered and crafted disappearing stay, a hallmark of high quality.

Flat top, low profile steamer trunk with extra wide hardwood straps, steel banding, lip and hardware. This trunk looks a bit rough, but notice the brass lock and lock plate; the latches are especially nice and hard to find in good condition. The addition of the tapered clamps coming down from the lid and up from the bottom, and the reinforced corners are also marks of a nicer trunk.
Ca. 1895.
Value **$125-$250**

Front view of low profile steamer, showing metal lid lifter, brass lock and lock plate, and the exceptionally nice latches in working order.

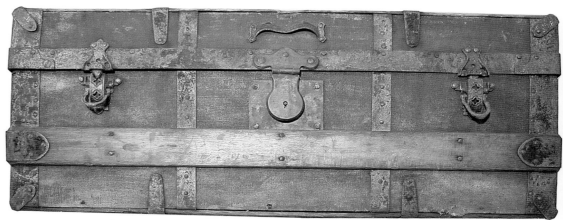

Detail of brass lock and lock plate.

Detail of latch, well styled, but the spring mechanism is vulnerable and often found broken.

Detail of latch with molded lift.

Flat top steamer with hardwood slats, tin corner trim, steel banding and hardware with a brass-plated lock. This trunk was an economy model in its day, however, the built in lifts add a nice touch, and it is a good candidate for refinishing.
Ca.1900.
Value: **$100-$150**

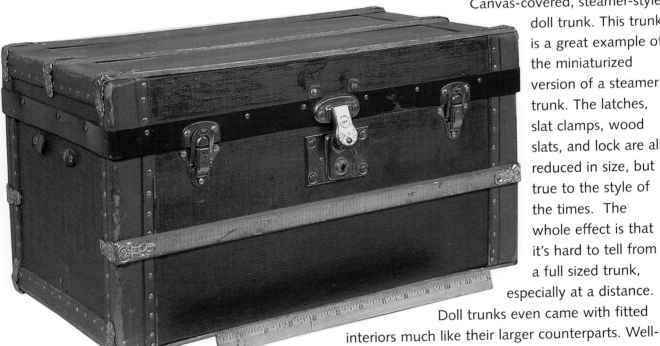

Canvas-covered, steamer-style doll trunk. This trunk is a great example of the miniaturized version of a steamer trunk. The latches, slat clamps, wood slats, and lock are all reduced in size, but true to the style of the times. The whole effect is that it's hard to tell from a full sized trunk, especially at a distance. Doll trunks even came with fitted interiors much like their larger counterparts. Well-made, well-proportioned doll trunks are somewhat scarce.
Ca. 1900.
Value: **$150-$300**

Early automobile trunk. This trunk was constructed with a stepped back so that it could be fitted up against the back of an auto. It also has leather straps to tie it down to the vehicle. The front opens up to reveal a number of removable suitcase-like compartments, each with their own handles, latches, and locks. It is covered with leather and has all brass hardware.
Ca. 1900.
Value: **$600-$1,200**

A view showing the multi-case interior of the automobile trunk.

Well-built low profile steamer trunk. The pine body is covered with canvas, the straps are of hardwood, and the hardware is brass plated. Notice the lid lifters built into the latches and the addition of the guides on either side of the lock.
Ca.1900.
Value: **$125-$300**

Interior view of low-profile steamer with covered tray.

Detail of latch with lifter and fancy brass-plated corners.

Detail of leather handles with original end caps.

High-quality flat top steamer trunk made by Henry Likly & Co. A pine body is covered with brown canvas, and the slats are of oak. The lip is made of steel and the latches, guide, and lock brass plated, but the slat clamps and corners are iron. The trunk originally had leather straps that wrapped around the body and buckled in the front, guided by leather keepers. The missing lock hasp detracts a bit from the value, but it is a style that is not hard to find. Ca.1905.

Value: **$150-$350**

Detail of cast iron slat clamp.

Close up of brass maker's tag attached to the top of the trunk. Henry Likly & Co., Rochester, NY.

Anne Morse

Painted metal-covered doll trunk. This doll trunk is painted with a checkerboard pattern, over a metal exterior. The pattern is a repeated black and opalescent gray. And it has all of the appropriate small-sized hardware including latches, lock, and corners. Ca.1910.

Value: **$125-$250**

Flat top, canvas-covered steamer trunk, with hardwood slats. The corners are trimmed with tin, and the lip, corners, and latches are made of steel. The lock and plate are brass plated. The wraparound leather straps are guided by leather strap keepers.
Ca.1910.
Value: **$150-$350**

European flat top steamer.
During this period, the Europeans were in the vanguard of innovation with wood.
This trunk is made with birch plywood that has been steamed and bent in a mold to form the curved edges. The high-ribbed hardwood slats are unique to European trunks, and are also made with the steaming and bending process. This trunk is covered with a heavy canvas that has been painted to look like embossed leather. It has leather banding along the edges and solid brass fittings. It also has two fancy solid brass locks. This type of trunk can be found in all sizes from suitcase all the way up through wardrobe. The quality can also vary considerably, with some trunks having brass plated fittings and one lock.
Ca. 1910.
Value: **$150-$400**

Later model wardrobe trunk. This is a heavy-duty wardrobe trunk made of plywood with a pressed cardboard covering, which is often referred to as "vulcanized" or treated to withstand the weather. The corners, latches, and lock are brass-plated steel. These trunks were made to endure endless miles of travel on ships and railroads, and rough handling by dockworkers. Mildew on the interior of this type of trunk is very hard to remove and reduces the value by at least half. Ca. 1925.
Value: **$250-$500**

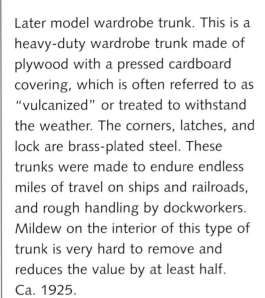

Interior view. Blue cloth-covered interior, with graduated drawers on the right side, and with hangers and slack bar on the left. This is a fairly common interior, although wardrobes interiors vary and the higher-end models of their day were fancy and elaborate.

Wardrobe steamer trunk. This W.W. Winship wardrobe trunk features all brass hardware and multiple compartments. Wardrobe trunks were produced on a grand scale until about 1935. As the mode of transportation changed from ships and trains to cars and planes, so did the method of transporting personal goods. Trunks got left behind. Wardrobes were sort of the last gasp of trunks. Big, lumbering, and unwieldy, they were built of wood, cardboard, cloth, and steel, and needed a two-wheeled dolly or several strong-backed porters to move. They also came in many qualities, some thin as a wafer, others, luggage of lords. Be wary of wardrobes that have any type of odor or mildew smell, as it is very difficult and costly to get rid of.

Ca. 1925.

Value: **$300-$800**

Wardrobes Ca. 1895 and later.

Value:

Low quality: **$250-$700**

Average: **$750-$1,200**

Highest quality: **$1,500-$4,000+**

Open view showing the multiple compartments and drawers. Note the original wood hangers.

Canvas-covered, low profile, flat top steamer trunk. This is an example of a later model steamer trunk. While it is well built with good quality hardware, it shows the direction that trunks had taken by the time it was made. The edging, once leather on these trunks, is now pressed cardboard or "leatherette." All of the hardware is brass plated. The body is made of plywood and the oak slats are very slim. Even though the materials have changed, this trunk was built for rough handling and inclement weather.
Ca. 1925.
Value: **$125-$250**

Flat top steamer trunk, covered with painted pressed cardboard. This steamer trunk has original brass plated latches, lock, clamps, and leather handles.
Ca. 1935.
Value: **$50-$125**

Antique Trunks

Sandy Speier

Wardrobe trunk with ribbed exterior. The exterior of this trunk was made to look like corrugated steel, when in fact it's corrugated pressed cardboard that has been painted. Nevertheless, it is a trunk built for rough handling and long passages. Notice the slight dome on the top of the trunk. This was added so that the trunk would not be stood on the wrong end, causing the hanging clothes to fall.
Ca. 1925.
Value: **$400-$600**

Price Guide

Value

At home, trunks served as the keepers of most valued possessions and family records.

How do you determine the value of a trunk? As you may suspect, there are a number of factors that determine the value of a trunk. Age, condition, maker, style, and, of course, how badly do you want it. You will notice in the price guide that a trunk can be worth just a few dollars or as much as several thousand dollars.

Very few trunks are worth nothing. Most have at least some value in their hardware. Antique locks, latches, hinges, and so forth are not that easy to come by and it's always a good idea, if you are working with trunks, to pick up parts trunks when you can. A parts trunk is just that. Not good enough to repair or restore but useful for the parts it has. For example, a good solid brass lock would be worth $25-50, latches $5-10 each, hinges $3-5 each. And that is just the basic stuff. There are brass buttons, wood from the body, trays, and many other useful pieces and parts.

The best way to figure out the value of parts is to look in a trunk parts catalog and price the individual parts. You will probably determine that if you were to add up all of the parts used on a trunk it would total in the $100 to $150 range. And that's not counting the wood body of the trunk, which can also be useful if you are doing refinishing work.

But how do you tell the $50 trunk from the $5,000 trunk? Well, trunks, like everything else, have all different levels of quality. Look first for a label. Is it a Louis Vuitton or a Neverbreak? Compare the label with what you know about the maker and that will start you on the road to value. But don't use the name alone as a final factor in determining the value. Louis Vuitton made quite a few fairly low quality trunks in the late 19th century. There are some flat top steamers with the LV label that are only on a par with P&S, U.S. Trunk Company, or any number of mediocre makers. They are just plain steamers without brass hardware or any other fancy fittings. However, even those cheapie Vuittons would be worth quite a bit more than their American counterparts chiefly because of the name. But they wouldn't approach the multi-thousand-dollar level of the better Vuitton trunks. Brass hardware, zinc bottoms, linen interiors, and multi trays are all signs of high quality.

If the trunk is fitted with heavy-duty, sometimes ornate hardware, that's usually a good sign that the maker wanted to produce a quality product. This adds value. Other factors: Cast corners are better than stamped. Look for solid brass hardware rather than brass plated or iron, and good solid rollers on the bottom, or rollers that wrap around the end. A stay that disappears inside a slot when closing is an excellent example of high-quality workmanship.

Cloth interior instead of paper will raise the quality as well as good looking brass locks, the fancier the better. Compartments in the lid and one or more trays will also add value to a trunk.

Other things to consider when determining the value are the design elements of the trunk. Dome top trunks are generally more desirable than flat top trunks. Of course there are exceptions to this. Louis Vuitton made very few dome top trunks. In fact, I've never seen one. And a good LV flat top is worth far more than just about any dome top that you can name. But LV aside, the dome tops are considered to have more of a pleasing shape and are in greater demand than flat tops. That's really the only reason. They aren't "better" trunks in the way they are put together or because of the hardware.

You will always want to weigh in with the condition of the trunk when considering the value. Is it like new, some wear, or falling apart? There are many problems a trunk can develop over the years, from broken or rusted parts to mildew and rotted wood. Most problems can be fixed, but they will all exact a price.

Condition Guide: Use this condition guide along with The Valuerator System® that follows to help determine the value of your trunk.

This is a five-part condition guide of a trunk with No. 1 being the best and No. 5 being the worst.

1. The trunk is in mint condition. This means that all it needs is a careful, perhaps even professional, cleaning. There are no rips, tears, or broken parts. If it had a tray originally, it is still there. All the hardware is intact and functional and it even has the original handles. The lock works and it would be nice if the key is with the trunk. It can have initials or travel labels on it. If it is covered with leather, that is not dried or torn. If it is painted, the paint is in excellent condition and the colors are strong. Whatever the covering, it is in excellent condition. In other words, if you went to a store to buy a new trunk, this is what you would find.

2. The trunk is in excellent condition. The handles are probably missing or broken. The tray may be missing. There may be tears or breaks in the covering that can be easily repaired. Perhaps a button or two are missing. Physically, the trunk is sound and most all of the hardware is there and working. There may be some minor staining that can be cleaned, and little or no rust on the hardware and metal trim. There is no mildew on the canvas covering. Paint is in very good condition. Interior is very clean with no mildew or stains. This is a trunk that is a candidate for restoration and can be brought back to original condition with careful work.

3. Good, sound, used condition. This trunk has been around. It is physically sound but has a number of problems. The handles are broken or missing. Hinges may be bent or broken. Interior is stained, ripped, partly, or all missing. Lock missing, jimmied, or otherwise broken. Rusted metal, missing tray, broken wood, tattered covering, and mildew all add up to make this trunk a No. 3. This is a good candidate for refinishing. To do so you would remove the rest of the covering and refinish the wood underneath. It is also a borderline candidate for restoration. It would really depend on the maker, the rarity, and the overall quality of the trunk.

4. Well used condition. All of the problems of a No. 3 plus it may have a rotted bottom, missing hardware, broken body, and other problems both major and minor. While this trunk is beyond restoration it could most likely be refinished with some major repairs.

5. This trunk is so badly deteriorated that it is only good for use as a parts trunk. It still has value in the parts that remain. Wood slats, lock and latches, hinges, and other hardware all give this trunk value. If you are working on a trunk, some parts, such as locks and latches, are very hard to find. Most any trunk is worth $25 for the parts.

Valuing a refinished trunk:

It's a bit more difficult to attach a value to a trunk that has been refinished. The reason is that there are many levels to which a trunk can be refinished. We've seen some trunks that have been refinished so badly they actually decrease in value. This is really hard to do but some refinishers seem to have achieved it. A gritty or oily surface, splotchy paint, hairs from the canvas sticking out are all signs of a poorly refinished trunk. Badly sanded repairs, or overlooked cracks and breaks, also detract from the value of the trunk. Repairs poorly done or not done at all are usually the result of lack of knowledge, not caring, rushing, or just not paying attention to the details.

Interiors of a refinished trunk also can run the gamut from not done at all to very well done. Look for poorly applied liner with misaligned patterns or liner that is coming loose. The interior may be finished with cloth or wood. If it is, look for poorly aligned or split wood sections. Stained or torn cloth liners will also detract.

On the other hand, a well refinished trunk can be worth many times what it was worth in the rough. A typical canvas-covered, flat top steamer trunk in used condition can be purchased in the New England area for $40 to $195. If it is well refinished, it can then be sold for $600 to $700 or more. We see refinished trunks in antique shops all the time. The price is generally $200 to $400, and price usually reflects the quality of the refinishing job. These would be classified as mediocre and have some or all of the problems mentioned above.

So if you are buying a trunk that has been refinished, expect to pay according to the type of job that was done. But keep in mind that if you do buy a trunk that has been badly refinished and want to have it redone, it may actually cost more than a trunk that was never touched. Because what has been badly done will need to be undone before it can be refinished properly.

The Valuerator System®:

The following is our unique points system called "The Valuerator System®" to help with figuring out the value of your trunk. Use this points system in conjunction with the condition guide above to help determine the value of your trunk.

The Valuerator System®:

• **Quality:** High quality maker such as Louis Vuitton, Gillmore, Haskell, Goyard, etc. The better the maker, the more points you add. From 1 to 5 points with 5 being the best.

Points_____

• **Condition:** Add 1 to 5 points according to condition. Add 5 points if the trunk is in No. 1 condition, 4 points if in No. 2, etc.

Points_____

• **Age:** The older a trunk, the more points. Figure this by dividing up the years 1780-1930 into five parts. Starting with 1930 and going backwards add 1 point for every 30 years.

Points_____

• **Style:** Trunks are desired according to their style in the following order: Dome tops, embossed metal covered, curve tops, flat tops, low profile, plain metal covered, wardrobes. Add 1 to 5 points for style with 5 points going to dome tops.

Points_____

• **Unusual features:** Half trunks, theatrical trunks, compartments in the lid, extra tray, brass banding, large brass buttons, or any feature not found on the average trunk. Add 1 point for each feature.

Points_____

Add up the points that you have and if the total is 21 or more, then value your trunk at the high end of the Value estimate in the price guide. The fewer points you have, the lower down on the Value estimate your trunk will fall. If it goes below 5 points, it's probably a parts trunk.

Total Points_____

21 or more: Your trunk goes to the head of the price pile.
15-20:   Your trunk is pretty darned good but not the best.
10-14:   You have a valuable trunk, well worth restoring.
5-9:   Your trunk is salvageable and worth working on but will probably need a lot of work.
0-4:   Most likely a parts trunk.

Value

Buying

The Captain comes ashore with his well-traveled trunk.

Buying a trunk can be an experience that you will always remember. There are many ways to purchase a trunk: auction, yard sale, flea market, antique show, antique shop. Prices will vary according to the trunk, the location, and the people selling.

Auction

If you are buying at an auction, you will probably want to follow the old saying "caveat emptor" or buyer beware. Just what does that mean? It means that most things sold at an auction are sold "as is." If there is a problem with the trunk, it's up to you to find out just what it is before you buy. Broken hinges, missing lock, cracked top, whatever the problem, determine if the condition will keep you from buying the trunk before you bid. This means arriving early enough at the auction to look the trunk over and decide if it's something for you.

At this point, don't underestimate the amount of work that will be involved to restore or refinish the trunk. Some people will do this in order to justify the purchase at a higher price. If you want to pay a lot more than the trunk is worth because you like it, that's another thing and it's OK to do. In either case, now is the time to decide what your maximum bid will be. Once the auction starts, the heat of the moment can carry you along and, if you don't have a limit, you might be tempted to overbid. You often hear about auction records being set. Frequently, this is just what happens.

When the trunk comes up for bid, there are several tactics you might follow. One is to wait while the auctioneer tries to get a bid started at a higher price. If no one bids, he or she will keep lowering the price until someone does bid. You can let the auctioneer lower the price until you want to jump in and, hopefully, you will get the trunk at a much lower price. However, this tactic may backfire as people seeing the trunk drop in price may want to jump into the fray. Then there will be more competition to drive the price higher. Another tactic is to start off high or at the asking price. The idea here is to show others you are serious about this item and "scare off" the other bidders. Sometimes it works but not always. In any case, be sure to stop bidding when you reach your limit. There will be other trunks coming along if you miss out on this one.

People sometimes buy trunks solely for the contents. You might ask someone who is bidding against you if that is the case. If so, you could offer them a reasonable price for the trunk alone and they would keep the contents.

Antique shop/flea market

If an antique shop or flea market is the place where you buy, you will have to approach the purchase in a different manner. You will be dealing one on one with the owner of the trunk and this can often work to the benefit of both parties. As at the auction, you will want to look the trunk over and determine the condition and costs or time for repairs or restoration.

Most dealers have flexibility with prices. There is the asking price or the price on the tag and then there is the so-called dealer discount, which is more or less the automatic deduction that is given to anyone who asks. This is usually around 10 percent. And there is the final selling price.

Here is one scenario for buying at a shop or flea market: You see a trunk you like, determine the price and condition, and decide what is the most you will pay. You would generally ask the dealer if they could "do any better" on the item. Or if they have given you a price you might ask, "Is your price firm?" You can use words to that effect, but remember to be polite and keep a good humor. Some people criticize or run down the item in order to try getting a better price: "It's chipped here, rusted over there," etc. The dealer usually knows the condition of the article and may be put off by this approach.

I often use just the opposite tact. I praise the merchandise and point out the good things. This usually sets a friendly tone, puts the merchant more at ease, and paves the way to a better price. After the merchant has set a "best price," you can either make your decision then or you have the option to make an offer. If the price the merchant has quoted is higher than what you want to pay, then make an offer that would be perhaps just a little lower than your highest price. The reason for this is that bargaining is a give and take game and you will want to leave the other person a little room to maneuver. After you have made your offer, the merchant can accept it, reject it and stick with their price, or offer to meet you half way. Chances are if you have made it this far, you will probably make a purchase.

Yard or tag sales

Prices at yard sales or estate tag sales are generally low enough to allow buying without too much bargaining. However, you might want to follow the same tactics as at the antique shop. Make an offer. The owner can accept, reject, or counter-offer. They will very rarely strike you with a cane. Be polite and of good humor. As my grandmother used to say, "You can catch more flies with honey than you can with vinegar."

Another question: Why are you buying a trunk in the first place? To use? To give away? To resell, refinish, restore? Firewood? These factors all enter into the price you are willing to pay. While quality and condition will be the two strongest factors, you will want to give consideration to your ultimate goal. If you are buying to resell, you will need to consider profit. If you are buying a present for someone, you might be willing to pay a little more.

If you are buying for your own collection, then it gets a little more complicated. Here's why: If you are making an investment in a collection that you plan to dispose of at a later date, you will want to focus on the very best trunks that you can buy: trunks that are of the highest quality; trunks that are rare; trunks that are in very good condition. Of course, there will be exceptions. But on the whole, you would want to follow those guidelines. If those are the types of trunks you are looking for, you will most probably not find many bargains. Still, you will never regret paying a little more for a good trunk. Just as with any antique, values will go up faster for the better trunks.

Disclaimer: I only encourage you to consider these trunks for purchase. I do not actually urge you to buy them. Yes, I know, never use the word "investment" when it comes to antiques. Buy it because you like it, is the catchphrase. Not invest-ment. But the fact is many collectors buy antiques with reselling at a later date in mind. And if you are one of those collectors, then I urge you to choose wisely. And that involves looking at which items are currently rising in value the fastest and which items you believe will go up in the future.

Reselling a trunk can also cost you a percentage of the value of the trunk: as much as 30 percent to 50 percent in some cases. It would depend on how you sell. At auction, plan to pay at least 10 percent commission. From an antique shop on consignment, plan to pay 20 percent to 30 percent or more commission. Wholesale to a dealer, plan to be paid 40 percent to 60 percent of the value of the trunk.

Here, then, are some trunks to consider buying for investment or other purposes.

Hide-covered trunks: These are the earliest trunks one is apt to come across. Built from the late 18th into the early 19th centuries, these trunks came in many shapes and sizes. They were covered with untanned hides. Hair and all. Hardware usually consisted of hand-forged iron handles and latch-style lock. They were decorated individually with small brass tacks around edges. Some were more elaborate than others, with initials on top surrounded by an oval of tacks. In addition, some have wonderful makers' labels still intact.

Jenny Lind trunks in original condition: Jenny Lind trunks, which can be easily identified by their unique keyhole or hourglass shape, are rare to begin with and many of the ones you see around have been refinished. If you can find one in close to original condition, then that would be a good buy. If it has brass clad steel banding, so much the better. That would add about 25 percent or more to the value. These trunks had compartments in the lid and trays. It would be nice if they were still there. While mildew is still a factor with this type of trunk, it's not the problem that it is with a wardrobe because the interior of a Jenny Lind is not very complex.

Oak slat trunks: Very few of these trunks were made and fewer still survive. They were made for a short period of time, from about 1865-1875. You will want to consider paying a premium for this type of trunk no matter the condition. These are among the rarest of trunks. They were usually fitted with compartments in the lids and fancy trays. These were the only trunks that were never covered with leather, cloth, metal, or paper. The entire bodies were covered with oak slats and the tops are either curved or domed.

Haskell Brothers, Goyard, Gillmore: These three trunk makers all made trunks of the highest quality. They are all on the same level as Louis Vuitton, but not nearly as well known. These trunks are actually in shorter supply than Louis Vuittons because Vuitton has remained in business all these years while Haskell and Gillmore have not. If you can find them, you can usually buy these trunks at a fraction of the price of a Louis Vuitton.

Pre Civil War Era trunks in original condition: Prior to the time of the Civil War, there were not that many trunks being made. Most of those trunks are hide covered with the hair still on the hide. They were made in small shops, and are currently under appreciated. Look for many different sizes and shapes: flat top, curved top. Nice if they have the original hand forged hardware.

Civil War Era trunks: A trunk from this period could be a good candidate for consideration if the leather, paper, or fabric covering is in near mint condition. Handles and hardware should also be intact. The more unusual examples of these trunks may be decorated with brass buttons or even brass strapping and fine locks.

Wardrobe trunks: Not many people consider this type of trunk because it is large and unwieldy. But we have seen a surge in interest in wardrobe trunks and believe that interest will continue to increase along with their value. Danger! Make certain that any wardrobe trunk you buy is free from mildew. It is extremely costly to rid a wardrobe trunk of mildew. The interior of this type of trunk is a complex mixture of cloth, wood, hardware, glue, and rivets, all of which must be removed and replaced to rid the trunk of mildew. Louis Vuitton, Goyard, Gillmore, Hartmann, and Oshkosh are a few of the better quality wardrobe trunk makers to consider. There were many other makers of good quality wardrobes and any that turn up would deserve a good inspection.

Additionally, any trunks with unusual characteristics: wall trunks, dresser trunks, trunks that fold out into a bed, and bevel top trunks. Examples of these trunks are shown in the price guide section. These are all rare trunks and will be in demand as people find out about them. Anything that gives the trunk an additional leg up will make it very collectible and more desirable.

Great buys

There are many thousands of trunks still in attics, barns, and cellars. Over the years they slowly make their way to auctions, flea markets, yard sales, and antique shops. Buying an antique trunk is one way to enter into the antique market on a budget.

Here are some of the buys we have found over the past five years or so:

- Curved top oak slat trunk purchased at the giant antique flea market in Brimfield, Mass.
  Cost: $295
  Value: $1,800
- Flat top Louis Vuitton trunk purchased from an antique shop in southern New Hampshire.
  Cost: $50
  Value: $3,500
- Dome top leather covered trunk purchased at an estate auction in New England.
  Cost: $45
  Value: $700

- Early flat top Crouch and Fitzgerald trunk with leather covering and brass buttons, purchased from a group shop in the Northeast.
  Cost: $35
  Value: $1,200
- Civil War Era bed trunk found at a flea market in Rowley, Mass.

  Cost: $385
  Value: $3,500

Not all the trunks that you will buy will have a purchase to value ratio of 1:10. As trunks become more popular, their prices will rise accordingly. Over the next 10 years, we expect the price of trunks to double or quadruple in many areas of the country. Even in New England, where trunks are still somewhat plentiful, prices will rise considerably.

Another venue for buying trunks is on the Internet. There are thousands of antique shops on the Internet. They are group shops, single owner shops, or auctions such as eBay. It's fairly easy to find trunks this way because instead of driving from shop to shop looking for that elusive dome top, you can just type the name into a search engine such as Google and it will do the work for you. You can also type in what you are looking for at the location itself. Many of the auctions and shops have their own search engine that will help you find what you are looking for.

Buying this way has both pluses and minuses. The plus is that you can save both time and money because you don't have to drive around or drive to a specific location looking for merchandise. You will also be able to view much more merchandise in a shorter period of time. The minus is that you can't handle the merchandise before you buy. It's pretty easy to doctor up a photograph to make something look better than it really is. You also will have to pay for shipping, which can add up to several hundred dollars for a large trunk.

If you do buy this way, be sure that you read and understand the seller's guarantee and return policy. If you are buying on eBay, be sure to read the seller's feedback, which is accessed by clicking on the number next to the seller's username. The feedback will give you some indication of how the seller is to deal with.

Basic Refinishing

Many craftsmen plied the trade of trunk maker. Repairing trunks was a full-time endeavor for many during the late 19th century.

<u>*Warning notice:*</u> Before you start refinishing a trunk, ask yourself what your goal is. Many trunks call for refinishing, i.e., removing what remains of the exterior covering and refinishing the wood underneath. However, there are plenty of trunks from which you would not want to remove the covering. These are rare, unusual, or early trunks. If a good looking item of furniture is what you are after, it's probably OK to go ahead. But if preserving the value of the trunk itself is your goal, then proceed with caution. You can actually destroy the major value of many trunks by removing the cover and refinishing. That type of trunk would call for restoration.

If you decide to refinish:

1. Clean the trunk using first a vacuum cleaner, then soap and water.

2. Clean the hardwood slats using denatured alcohol and steel wool. Make sure you have plenty of ventilation during this process because of the toxic fumes from the alcohol.

3. Now comes the metal trim. Wire brush, steel wool, and sand as needed to remove any rust or loose paint. Patch any bad spots in the metal trim. Find some thin sheet metal (you can use roof flashing found at any hardware store) and patch any holes or eroded spots on the outside. These patches will more or less disappear when you repaint the trim. Use the same type of nails that were used on the rest of the tin. Make sure that you hold a heavy piece of metal on the inside of the trunk when you hammer the nails in place for several reasons: a.) To keep from damaging the wood, and b.) So that the nail "clinches" or bends back into the wood as it comes through on the inside.

4. Remove the coverings from the trunk. Outside is usually canvas, leather, paper, or metal. Inside is usually a wallpaper type of material or a thin cloth. If it is metal covered, you would probably want to save it, as it's pretty hard to remove.

5. Next use a spray bottle to soak the wood. Remove all the glue, wash it off, wipe it down, and let it dry. Don't let it stay wet too long because the thin wood will warp.

6. Remove the covering from the interior, clean off all of the glue, and wash it with a 10 percent bleach solution to kill any mildew.

7. Seal the inside with several coats of oil based polyurethane. Make sure to have plenty of ventilation during this process because of the toxic fumes from the polyurethane. Paint the clinched over nails on the inside individually so they won't bleed through the liner.

8. Stain the outside wood. The slats are usually oak or some type of hardwood, so stain them a different color than the body of the trunk.

9. Add new handles. Use care taking off the handle end caps because the nails have probably been clinched over on the inside and if you pull them out without first straightening them, you risk damaging the wood. You can also make a tray for your trunk. Many had one or two trays and they are very useful.

10. Paint the metal trim and hardware using some type of rust resistant paint. We use a rustproof flat black paint. Polyurethane the wood on the outside with several coats of water based, satin finish urethane.

11. The last step will be to reline the inside with your choice of paper or cloth. And that's it.

Metal Covered Trunks, Refinishing

The procedure is much the same as for other trunks with the exception of how you treat the exterior metal covering the body of the trunk.

If your metal covered trunk is rusted or deteriorated:

1. Get rid of all the rust that you can, using a wire brush, steel wool, brass brush, and sand paper as needed. You can also use a wire wheel attached to a drill, but this calls for a little more experience because the spinning wire wheel can quickly eat up any wood it runs up against.

2. Next, sand down the wood slats.

3. Wash the whole thing with soap and water. Dry off with cloth or paper towels.

4. Find some thin sheet metal and patch any holes or eroded spots on the outside. Again, flat black paint used on the patches and metal trim will tend to cover up any new areas that you have spliced in.

5. Urethane the hardwood slats with several coats of water based satin finish urethane.

6. Paint the trunk body with your choice of color. A satin finish paint is preferred, as are the more subdued colors such as brick red, forest green, etc.

Warning: If you are using power tools, cleaning agents, or refinishing products such as paint and polyurethane, be sure to use proper safety measures. Consider using dust masks, goggles, and proper ventilation. Remember that you are dealing with lead paint and other harmful elements.

Metal Covered Trunks, Restoring

Metal-covered trunks in a nutshell.

If you have a metal-covered trunk in good condition, the best treatment is minimal treatment. You can apply oils or wax, but generally this will just attract dirt and dust. Additionally, wax needs maintenance; i.e. buffing, reapplying, occasional stripping, and then reapplying. An endless cycle. Just wash it with a very mild soap solution and then dry it. It leaves a nice, subdued patina. You may want to stabilize the cleaned exterior with two coats of satin finish, water based polyurethane.

Leather-Covered Trunks, Restoring

We treat leather-covered trunks minimally and with great care. Wipe off with a damp cloth and dry with a dry cloth. Use a leather treatment such as saddle soap to gently clean the leather, and shoe polish to give the leather color when needed and to blend in stains and worn spots. If the leather is stiff or crumbly, it may be too late. Trunks with the leather covering still intact are rare. From an antique lover's point of view, we find these nicely preserved leather trunks the real treasures. And worth noting, these 150 to 200 year old trunks in near original condition offer antique lovers the opportunity to own a very early piece for a few thousand dollars or less.

Mold or Musty Odor

If mold has gotten into the wood or lining of your trunk, here's how we usually deal with it:

1. Remove the lining from the inside of the trunk. Trunks are usually lined with paper or cloth. Sometimes this will almost fall off in your hands. Other times it is very difficult to remove, especially in certain cases where cardboard is used in the lid or base of the trunk and glued in.

2. After every trace of lining is removed, wash out the inside of the trunk with hot soap and water (something like Murphy's soap). If the mold is very strong you will want to use a mild bleach solution. Dry it with towels. Let it sit until it is completely dry. A little time in the sun won't hurt at this point, as sunshine is one of the best things for killing mold. But watch for warping because too long in the direct sunlight will cause the wood to buckle.

3. Now sand down the inside and vacuum it out.

4. Next, apply at least two coats of oil-based polyurethane, letting it dry between coats. You are now ready to reline your trunk and will not be bothered again by that musty odor.

Check out the resources section in the back of this book for books on refinishing trunks and sources for trunk parts.

Basic Refinishing

Trunk Makers Labels

You can never have enough trunks, so it's best to start at an early age, especially if you have travel plans.

Many trunk makers put labels in their trunks. Some of them are very plain and only one or two colors. Others are fancy with scrolls, fancy writing, and etchings of the trunks produced by the maker. Some of them go into great detail about what articles the maker produced. They would often have a listing such as: trunks, satchels, handbags, saddlery, boots, and shoes produced by one outfit.

Over the past 25 years, we have collected dozens of these labels. We have either taken pictures of them as they appear in a trunk or we have actually removed them from the trunks, scanned them into our computer, and repaired them with special software.

This has given us the opportunity to build up a sizable collection of antique trunk makers' labels that are rarely, if ever, seen. We have included several dozen of those labels in this book.

Makers' labels

Over the years there have been thousands of trunk makers. Many had their own labels printed, which they would then glue into the trunks they made. The label was often attached to the inside of the lid or inside back of the trunk. Sometimes the label would be attached to the bottom of a tray. Other labels were made of stamped metal and these were generally attached on the outside, either on the lid or the front of the trunk.

Most of the labels were very plain with basic information on them. The makers' names and sometimes their addresses were included. Other labels went into great detail about where the factory was located and other specific information about the company. Some such as Molloy had several paragraphs of information on the label as well as drawings of the styles of trunks produced. Labels with a lot of information like that are very useful in helping to attribute a certain trunk to a specific maker even if it doesn't have a label.

Some labels, such as Taylor and Leatheroid, carried guarantees or warranties as well as serial numbers. Some were printed in two or more colors and are quite fancy.

Unfortunately, time and wear and tear have taken their toll on many of these labels and they are often found in various states of disrepair, much as the trunk they are in. Some have been lost altogether. Others are partially torn or missing. Some have been covered with a new lining and can be recovered.

If you are refinishing or restoring a trunk and relining the interior in the process, there are a number of ways that you can deal with the label if it is still there.

You can work around the label. Remove the rest of the interior material but leave the label alone. It may need a bit of regluing or you may want to go over it with polyurethane to stabilize it.

If you need to remove it, do so slowly. Very slowly. Some labels may come off easily, especially if they are put on a canvas or linen lining. If the lining is paper, the label is much more difficult to remove.

Start by spraying with water and give it a good soaking. Let it stand for 15 or 20 minutes and see if you can start peeling up a corner. Be very careful and go about it slowly, because the paper is very fragile when it is wet and very easy to tear or split. You may have to work the label up a little at a time and keep spraying it to keep it wet.

Sometimes a putty knife is helpful in working the label up. It may actually take several hours of soaking, waiting, prying, and pulling to get the label off.

After it's off, lay it on a piece of absorbent paper and let it dry. At this point there are several options. One is to iron the label flat with a steam iron and reattach it. If the label has been torn or is in several pieces, you may want to glue it onto another piece of paper before reapplying it to the trunk. If the label is torn or missing some sections, one option is to scan it into a computer and repair it with a program such as PhotoShop and reprint it.

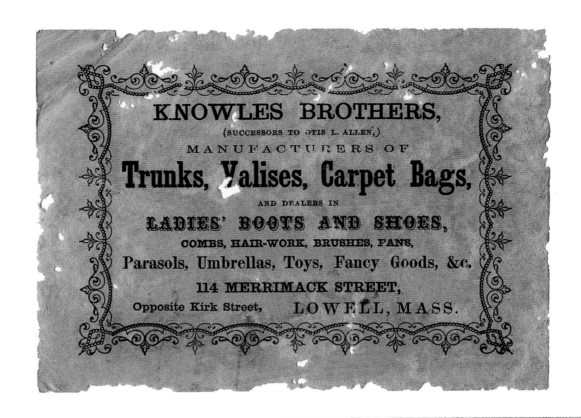

KNOWLES BROTHERS,

(SUCCESSORS TO OTIS L. ALLEN,)

MANUFACTURERS OF

Trunks, Valises, Carpet Bags,

AND DEALERS IN

LADIES' BOOTS AND SHOES,

COMBS, HAIR-WORK, BRUSHES, FANS,

Parasols, Umbrellas, Toys, Fancy Goods, &c.

114 MERRIMACK STREET,

Opposite Kirk Street,   LOWELL, MASS.

TRUNKS,
TRAVELLING BAGS,
Valices, Shoes, &c.,
Manufactured and sold, by
S. McLANATHAN,
No. 47 Merrimack Street,
LOWELL.

N. B. Old Trunks taken in exchange for new.
☞ Orders attended to at short notice. ☜

N. J. WHALEN.

MANCHESTER, N. H.

TRUNKS & HARNESS & COLLAR

EXTENSION CASES & HORSE CLOTHING

REPAIRING.   WHIPS & ROBES

CROUCH & FITZGERALD,

MANUFACTURERS,

Cor. Broadway & Maiden Lane,

AND

176 Chatham Street,

NEW YORK.

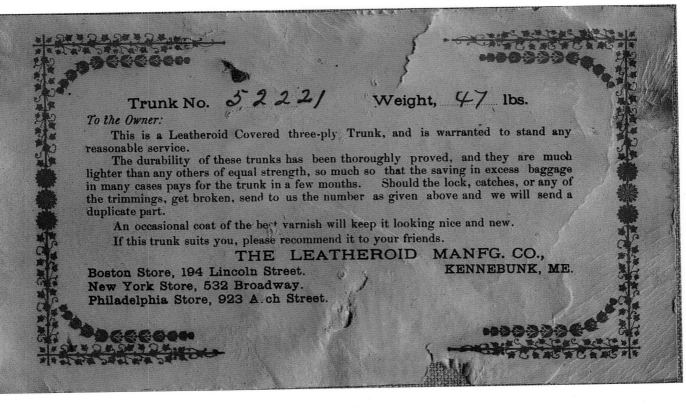

Trunk No. 52221   Weight, 47 lbs.

To the Owner:

This is a Leatheroid Covered three-ply Trunk, and is warranted to stand any reasonable service.

The durability of these trunks has been thoroughly proved, and they are much lighter than any others of equal strength, so much so that the saving in excess baggage in many cases pays for the trunk in a few months. Should the lock, catches, or any of the trimmings, get broken, send to us the number as given above and we will send a duplicate part.

An occasional coat of the best varnish will keep it looking nice and new.

If this trunk suits you, please recommend it to your friends.

THE LEATHEROID MANFG. CO.,
KENNEBUNK, ME.

Boston Store, 194 Lincoln Street.
New York Store, 532 Broadway.
Philadelphia Store, 923 Arch Street.

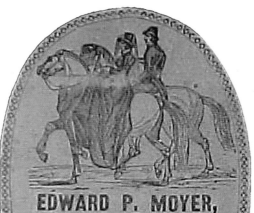

EDWARD P. MOYER,
SADDLE, BRIDLE,
HARNESS & TRUNK
MANUFACTURER,
Nos. 18 & 750 Market Street,
Sign of Golden Saddle No. 18,
PHILADELPHIA.

NATHAN NEAT,
SADDLE & TRUNK-MAKER,
4 & 5
ELM-STREET,
Opposite Jennings' Hotel,
BOSTON.

Henry Emmons, Printer, 743 Washington-Str.

THE M.G. LILLEY & CO.
MANUFACTURERS OF MILITARY & SOCIETY GOODS,
COLUMBUS.
OHIO.

EASTER & WINSHIP,

MANUFACTURERS OF

SOLE LEATHER AND EUGENIE

TRUNKS,

BAGS, VALISES, SATCHELS, &C

WHOLESALE AND RETAIL,

ELM STREET,

BOSTON.

CLINTON

Wall Trunk

Patented February 25, 1890.

MANUFACTURED SOLELY BY THE

CLINTON WALL TRUNK MFG. CO.

(INCORPORATED)

CLINTON, MASS.

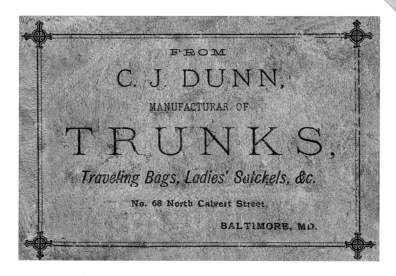

FROM

C. J. DUNN,

MANUFACTURAR OF

TRUNKS,

Traveling Bags, Ladies' Satchels, &c.

No. 68 North Calvert Street,

BALTIMORE, MD.

TRADE MARK

HASKELL BROS

TRUNK MANUFACTURERS CHICAGO

TELEPHONE 576.

52 MADISON STREET,

Three Doors East of State.

Sample Trunks and Cases

MADE TO ORDER.

Fine Sole Leather and Traveling Trunks

A SPECIALTY.

Factory, Nos. 13, 15 and 17 North Green St.

J. W. C. HASKELL.   J. E. HASKELL.

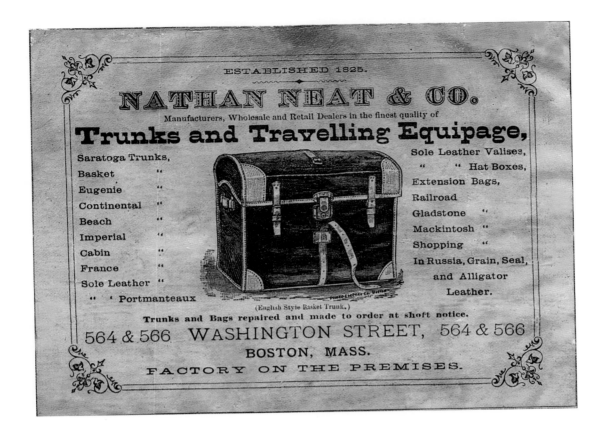

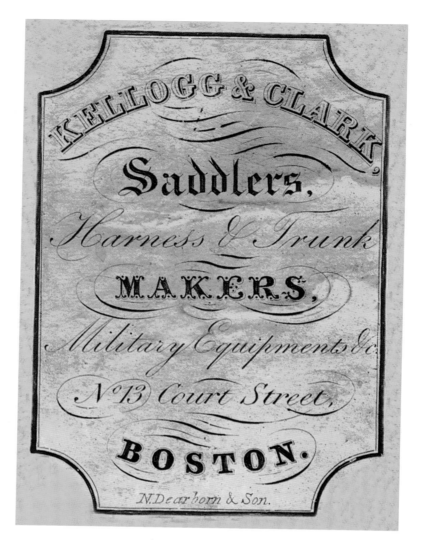

SAGE'S
❧ ❧ TRUNK DEPOT, ❧ ❧

628 & 630 Washington, Cor. Essex St., Boston, Mass.

JAMES L. TYLER,

Salesroom, No. 26 Avon Street, - - BOSTON,

Factory, No. 390 HANOVER STREET,

Manufacturer and Jobber of

TRUNKS AND BAGS.

—:—

Sole Leather Sample Cases and Sample Trunks on hand

AND MADE TO ORDER.

—:—

ESTABLISHED 1848.

MANUFACTURED AND SOLD BY

GEORGE MOLLOY,

15 MARKET STREET,
Lowell, Mass.

WHERE ALL KINDS OF

IRON, ZINC, CANVAS, DUCK AND CLOTH TRUNKS

May be found Cheaper than at any other establishment in Lowell.

Every Trunk made by Molloy has on it a Lock that the Keys of Trunks sold elsewhere will not unlock.

OLD TRUNKS TAKEN IN EX-
CHANGE FOR NEW ONES.
TRUNKS REPAIRED AND
LOCKS PUT ON AT
VERY REASONABLE PRICES.
LOCKS FOR SALE.
KEYS FITTED TO ALL KINDS
OF LOCKS.

ANY PATTERN OR STYLE OF
TRUNK DESIRED MADE
TO ORDER.
NO PAPER TRUNKS MADE
AT MOLLOY'S.
REMEMBER THE PLACE,
NEXT TO PUFFER'S
FURNITURE ROOMS,

No. 15 MARKET STREET.

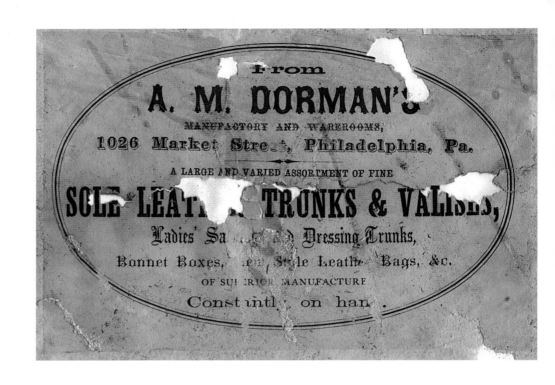

From

A. M. DORMAN'S

MANUFACTORY AND WAREROOMS,

1026 Market Street, Philadelphia, Pa.

A LARGE AND VARIED ASSORTMENT OF FINE

SOLE-LEATHER TRUNKS & VALISES,

Ladies' Saratoga and Dressing Trunks,

Bonnet Boxes, Sole Leather Bags, &c.

OF SUPERIOR MANUFACTURE

Constantly on hand.

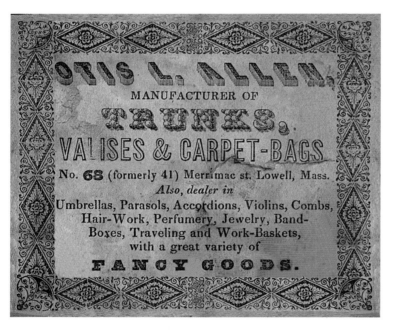

OTIS L. ALLEN,

MANUFACTURER OF

TRUNKS,

VALISES & CARPET-BAGS

No. 68 (formerly 41) Merrimac st. Lowell, Mass.

Also, dealer in

Umbrellas, Parasols, Accordions, Violins, Combs,
Hair-Work, Perfumery, Jewelry, Band-
Boxes, Traveling and Work-Baskets,
with a great variety of

FANCY GOODS.

EBENr HANCOCK

Saddler, Cap &
Harness, Trunk & Collar

MAKER.

Northampton

MASS.

Whips Matresses &c

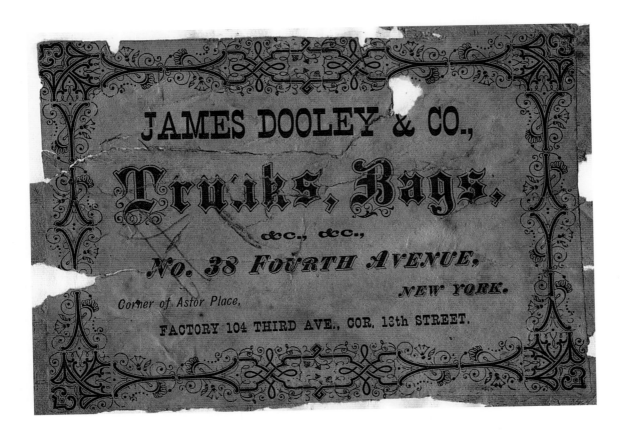

JAMES DOOLEY & CO.,

Trunks, Bags,

&c., &c.,

No. 38 FOURTH AVENUE,

NEW YORK.

Corner of Astor Place,

FACTORY 104 THIRD AVE., COR. 13th STREET.

TRADE MARK.
Strength, Lightness, Neatness,
and Comfort Combined.

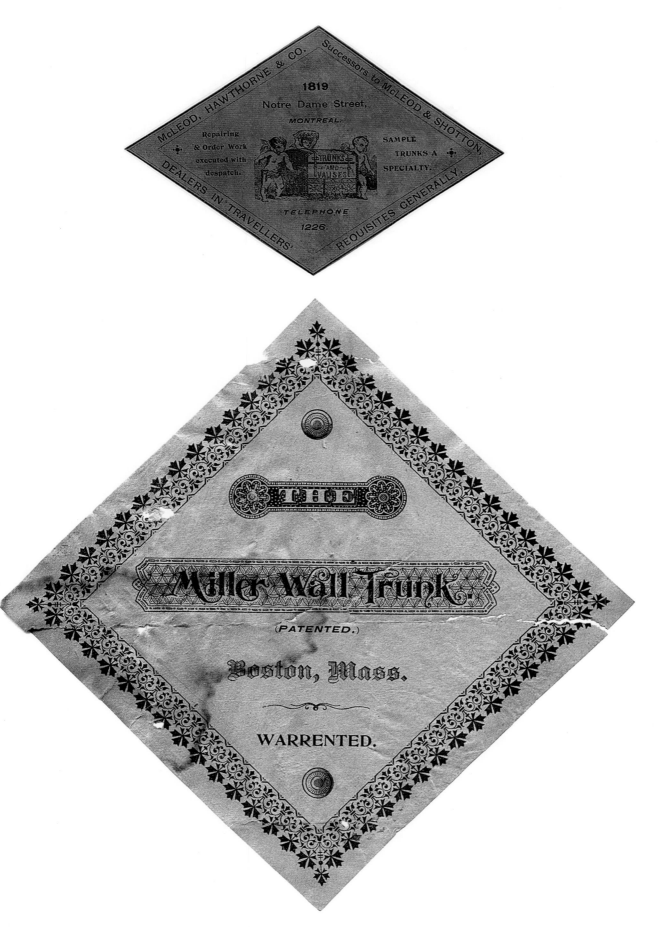

McLEOD, HAWTHORNE & CO.   Successors to McLEOD & SHOTTON,

1819
Notre Dame Street,
MONTREAL.

Repairing
& Order Work
executed with
despatch.

TRUNKS AND VALISES

SAMPLE
TRUNKS A
SPECIALTY.

DEALERS IN TRAVELLERS'   REQUISITES GENERALLY.

TELEPHONE
1226.

THE
Miller Wall Trunk.
(PATENTED.)
Boston, Mass.
WARRENTED.

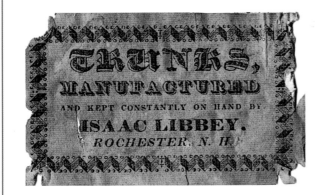

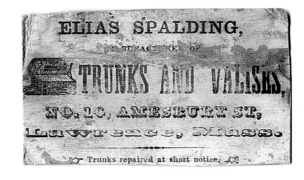

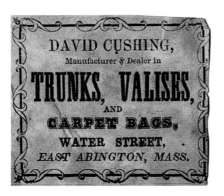

F. FALCONER & SON,
CHARLOTTE ST.
CARRIAGE, HARNESS AND TRUNK REPOSITORY.
HORSE FURNISHINGS   SHOE FINDINGS
SYDNEY. C. B.

FRANK A. STALLMAN,
MANUFACTURER OF
Stallman's Dresser Trunk.
THEATRICAL AND COMMERCIAL WORK.
57 East Spring St.   COLUMBUS, O.

U.S. TRUNK CO.
FALL RIVER, MASSACHUSETTS

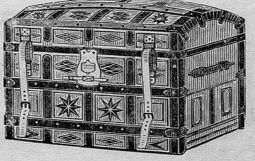

ALEXANDER McDONALD
MANUFACTURER OF
Sole Leather, Overland, Continental AND Light Weight
FRENCH TRUNKS

BASKET TRUNKS
STEAMER TRUNKS
LADIES' DRESS TRUNKS
GENTS' TRUNKS
AUTOMOBILE TRUNKS

STEAMER RUGS
DRESS SUIT CASES
GLADSTONE BAGS
ENGLISH KIT BAGS
SHIRT BOXES
HAT BOXES

ESTABLISHED 1852   15 BEACON ST., BOSTON, MASS.   TEL. 1946-4 HAY.

Trunk Maker's Labels

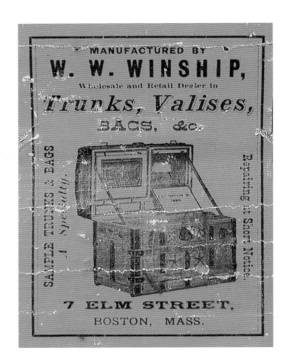

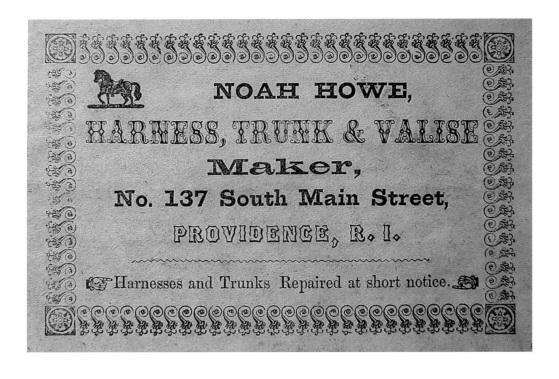

R. H. HAND,
TRUNK MANUFACTURER,
168 FULTON STREET, BROOKLYN,
AND
A COMPLETE ASSORTMENT OF
TRUNKS, VALISES, BAGS, &c.

N. B.—TRUNKS REPAIRED, OR TAKEN IN EXCHANGE.

LEONARD ROGERS,
Trunk Manufacturer,
NO. 272 PEARL-STREET,
TWO DOORS ABOVE BEEKMAN-SLIP,
New York:

MAKES and sells all kinds of TRUNKS.—Orders thankfully received and punctually executed.

September, 1813.

Printed by E. Low, No. 24 Catherine-st.

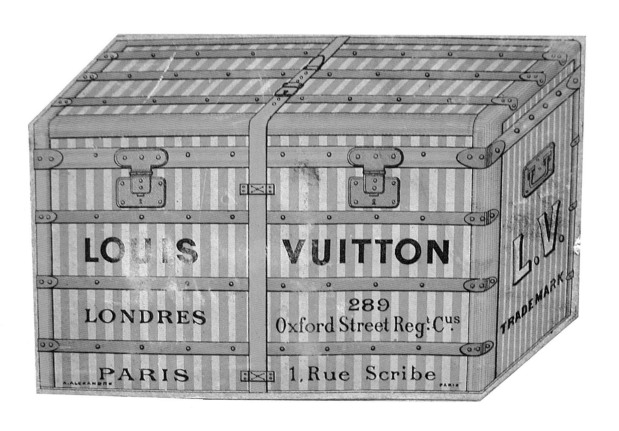

Locks

Trunks were used at home, when not traveling, and carried enchantments of days gone by

Most trunks had locks on them and locks are a good way to help identify the age or, in some cases, the maker of a trunk. The following section shows most of the common, and not so common, types of locks found on trunks arranged in a chronological order.

The earliest locks were usually made of hand forged iron. Some of these early locks had brass trim or a brass keyhole cover. As the years progressed, more parts of the locks were machine made, until about 1840 or so when the whole lock was made by machine from stamped and cast pieces.

Of course, there are exceptions to this. People didn't just stop making locks by hand in 1840. As with any new technology, there was a gradual transformation over a number of years. In fact, locks are still being made by hand today, especially in the Far East.

The locks in this section run the gamut from very fine, fancy brass locks to the cheaper locks made in the early 20th century.

There were many lock makers. Yale, Yale & Towne, Corbin, Long, and National were some of them. Some trunk makers had their own lock making facilities, but most makers bought locks from large manufacturers or at least had them custom made.

If you are looking for identification, the lock of a trunk is a good place to go. While there will rarely be the actual trunk maker's name on the lock, it will often have a patent date which is a very helpful start in identifying a trunk.

Locks can also present a problem sometimes. Especially on later trunks where the lock mechanism became more complex, it's a bit difficult to have a key made for them. If the trunk is not locked and there is no key, you have several options. You can take the trunk to a locksmith and have a lock fitted. Or you can remove the lock and then take it to the locksmith.

If the trunk is locked and you don't have a key, we would encourage you not to break the lock in order to open it. Many locks are very hard to replace and in some cases they are a valuable part of the trunk. If the trunk, indeed, is locked we would encourage you to take the trunk to a lock-smith and have it picked even if you don't have a key made. At least the lock will be intact. The

charge for picking is small. To have a key made is another story. Depending on the type of lock, the cost to have a key made could run from $5 to more than $100. It's also possible that the locksmith will decline to even try to make a key.

When it comes right down to it, ask yourself this question: "Do I really need a key for this trunk?"

If your trunk is missing the lock altogether, you might find a replacement lock at a flea market. You might also find a parts trunk that would have the right lock on it. You can study the trunks in this book to determine what type of lock yours had.

The most common problem with older locks is that the latch is missing. That's the long tongue that swings down from the lid into the lock. In most cases this is not a big problem. If the latch is missing, it's hardly noticeable and you probably would-n't want to go to the trouble of having one made.

This is a lock that was made from hand forged iron and stamped brass. It has a stamped brass keyhole cover with the word "Patent" stamped on it, indicating that the design was probably patented.
1820-1850

This is one of the earliest types of locks found on trunks. It is hand forged iron attached with handmade nails. These locks were not very fancy but they did have quite a lot of character. This one has a keyhole cover and the keyhole itself is a bit fancy. The latch is often missing from this type of lock and they are very hard to find.
1780-1840

A fancy stamped brass lock plate is the hallmark of this lock. The latch can't be seen because it's inside the lip of the lid.
1830-1855

This is a very fancy lock
with a sliding cast brass
dolphin keyhole cover.
The keyhole covers on this
type of lock very often are
missing. This is an extremely
rare lock to find and would
add tremendous value to the
trunk it is on.
1850-1860

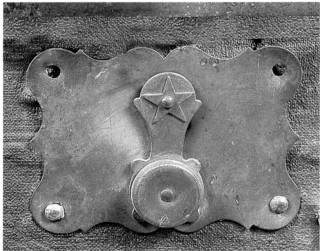

Another fancy brass lock with a mounted star
spring loaded keyhole cover. This type of lock is
most often found on Jenny Lind-style trunks.
1850-1865

This is a solid brass lock stamped out of a sheet of
very heavy metal. There are very few of this type
of lock around.
1865-1870

A fancy lock made of stamped brass. This is the type of lock that was used on the very best trunks. The latches on this kind of lock were often lost over the years.
1860-1870

This is a very plain brass lock found on a high-quality trunk, namely a Louis Vuitton. It has a dark patina on it that makes it look like steel or iron.
1860-1870

This lock is made from a combination of brass and steel. All of the components are machine made. 1860-1870

This plain steel and iron lock is made from stamped and cast components. The latch will often be missing. 1866-1875

This lock is a bit unusual with its heavy brass parts and the small pivoting keyhole cover. 1865-1875

This is a solid, heavy duty lock made from cast and stamped brass with steel workings inside. 1868-1875

A patent date on this lock of 1869 helps to zero in on the date that the trunk was made as well as the date the lock was made. The lock is attached to a high dome top, embossed zinc-clad trunk. It's quite a fancy lock and the trunk would have probably been rather expensive. Often gound missing the latch.
1869

Zinc plated steel locks were introduced in the early 1870s and were used on many trunks for the next twenty years or so.
1870-1890

Solid brass locks such as this one were always popular, especially on the better trunks. Most leather-covered dome top trunks were fitted with brass locks such as this one.
1870-1895

This lock was made with stamped steel and brass and was used for a few years in the late 19th century.
1885-1895

This solid brass lock was introduced in the early 1880s and was popular for many years. It has a much more complex locking mechanism than previous locks.
1880-1910

The French were very fond of brass as the material of choice for their locks.
1885-1895

This is a very unusual steel lock used for just a few years.
1890-1895

Another example of the popular brass lock with complex mechanism.
1890-1910

The Europeans strike again with their brass locks. This one being from Germany or Austria.
1890-1910

This all steel lock was one of the most popular locks produced and was used for many years by a lot of trunk makers.
1890-1930

The French just keep coming up with really nice looking brass locks, such as this Louis Vuitton example.
1890-1910

This is an all-steel lock that became the standard for most manufacturers.
1890-1930

Another example of the "standard" by a different maker than the previous one.
1890-1930

Not all of the later locks were cheapies. The better makers still took pride in their hardware, such as this lock used by Winship.
1910-1930

As trunk making tapered off, so did the quality of many locks. This is an example of how cheaply a lock can be made and still work.
1900-1935

Patents

Victorian Era peddlers found trunks handy to carry and to display their goods.

The current patent numbering system in the United States started on July 13, 1836, prior to which about 9,957 patents were issued between 1790 and 1836. These earlier patents were not originally numbered but have been assigned arbitrary numbers according to sequence. A fire destroyed almost 10,000 patent records on Dec. 15, 1836, of which 2,845 records were reconstructed. The rest of the patents were cancelled. Since that time, more than six million patents have been issued.

Sometimes a patent model was required to accompany the drawing, but in the case of trunks the drawings themselves were usually enough.

Many trunks have patent dates stamped on their hardware and that will give an indication when the trunk was made. When you are looking for a patent date on a trunk, look on the lock, rollers, latches, and slat clamps. These are the pieces of hardware where the date is usually stamped or has been included as part of the casting. The date will typically appear like this: "Mar1768." This can mistakenly be translated as March, 1768, and cause some confusion. However, we know there were no patents being issued in 1768. The date that is stamped is a shorthand method of saying "March 17, 1868."

If you see a patent date on a trunk, you will know that the trunk was made after that date, most likely within a year or two.

The following drawings are from the USPTO (United States Patent and Trademark Office) and accompanied applications for a patent by various trunk designers. We are showing here a representative sample of the many hundreds of trunk patents issued.

For more information on trunk patents, we suggest you go to the U.S. patent Web site: http://www.uspto.gov/go/classification/uspc190/sched190.htm

Class 190 is the patent office designation for trunks.

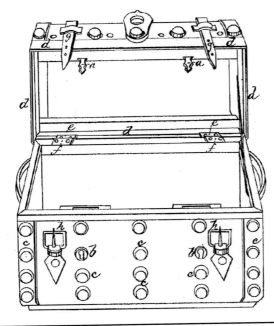

John Fitzgibbon devised a trunk with both hidden hinges and hidden lock to discourage unauthorized entry. It was invented in 1841.

Mathias Ludlum fashioned a water tight trunk in 1859.

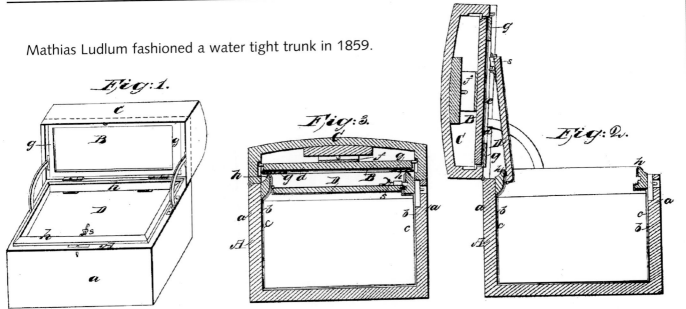

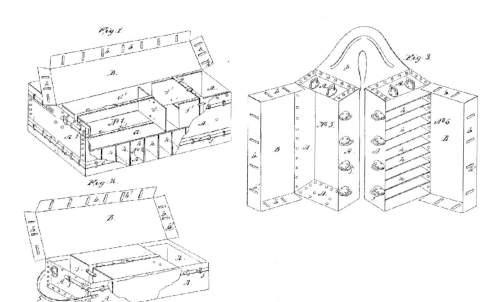

In 1863, Marshall Smith of St. Louis, Mo., invented a multi-compartment mail carrier.

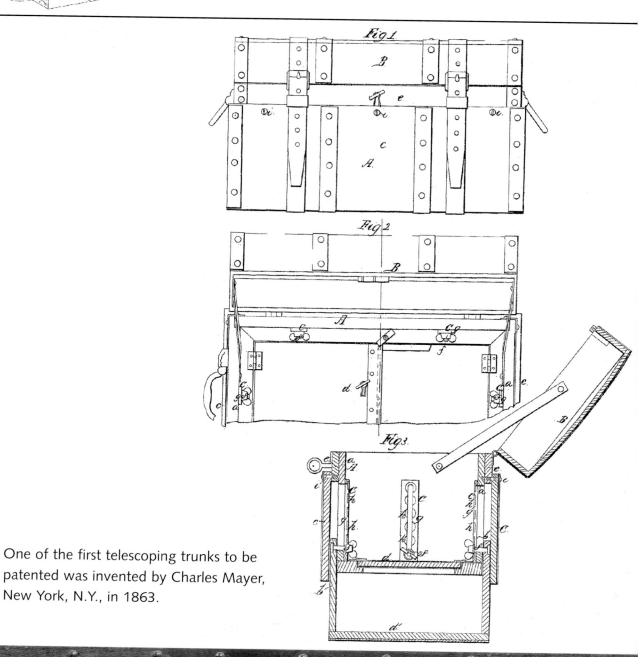

One of the first telescoping trunks to be patented was invented by Charles Mayer, New York, N.Y., in 1863.

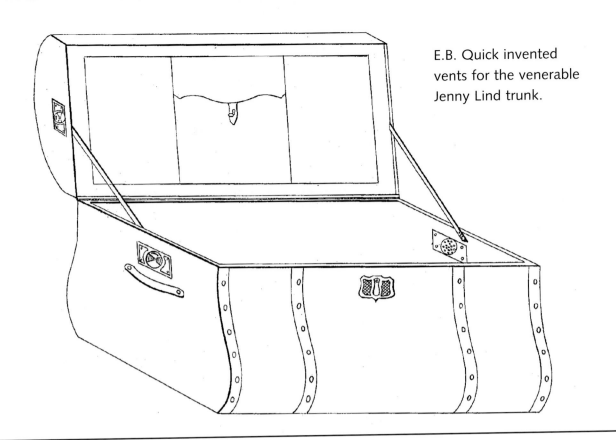

E.B. Quick invented vents for the venerable Jenny Lind trunk.

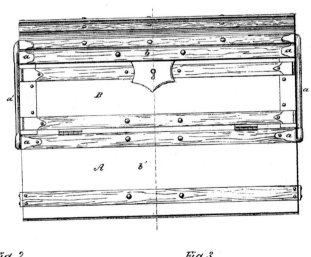

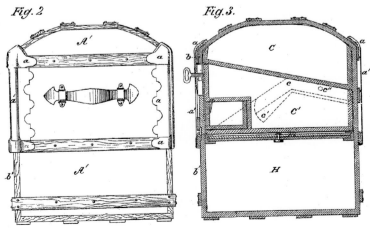

Fig. 2   *Fig. 3.*

Edward A.G. Roulstone of Boston, Mass., invented a trunk that opens from the front. The top stays put.

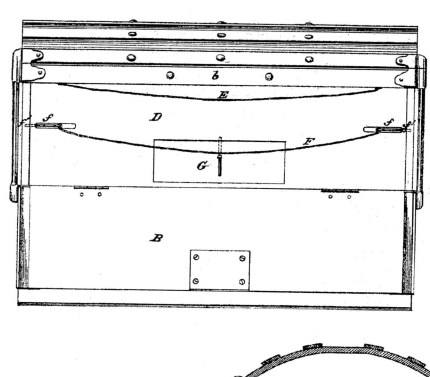

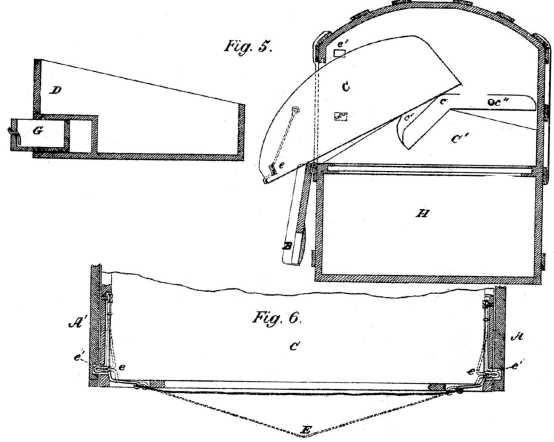

Fig. 5.

Fig. 6.

Another view of Roulstone's invention. Is this actually an improvement?

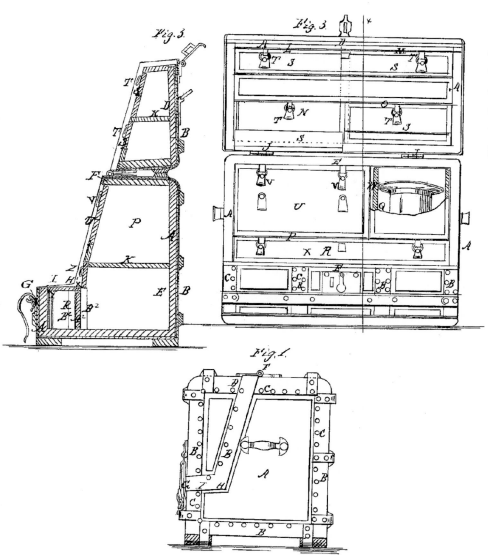

J.H. Burnett Jr. invented a dresser trunk in 1868. You could also push this trunk up against a wall and he thereby inadvertently invented a wall trunk.

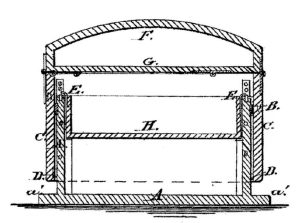
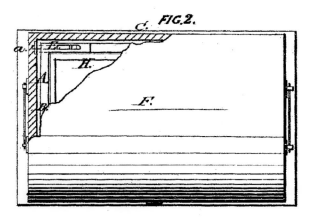

Henry Hickman of Omaha, Neb., devised a telescoping trunk in 1869. This trunk could be expanded upwards to accommodate more clothing or other articles.

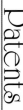

Patents

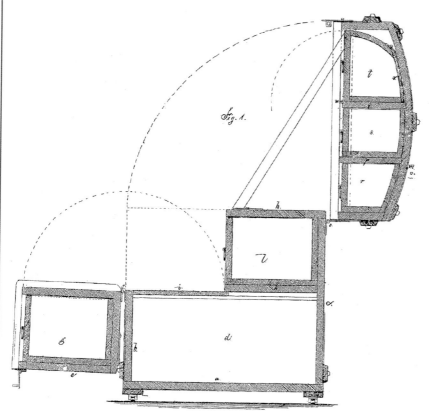

Thomas Hunt of New York, N.Y., invented a trunk in 1869 that could be opened in several ways so the articles contained therein could be reached without disturbing the other contents.

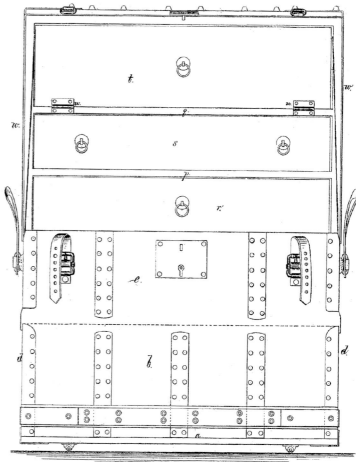

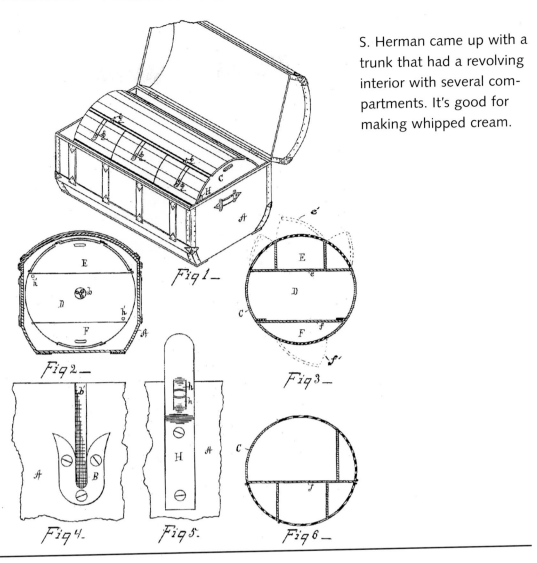

S. Herman came up with a trunk that had a revolving interior with several compartments. It's good for making whipped cream.

Fig 1—

Fig 2—

Fig 3—

Fig 4.

Fig 5.

Fig 6—

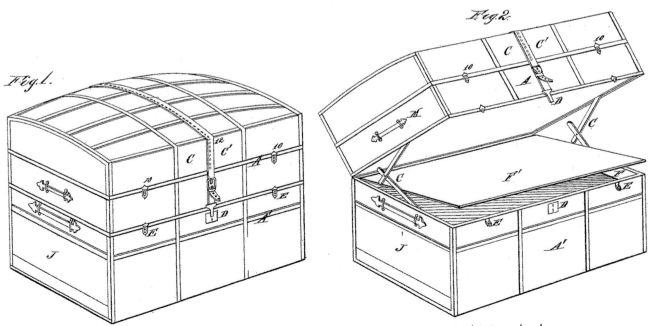

L. Singer was the inventor of this trunk that can be converted into a bed.

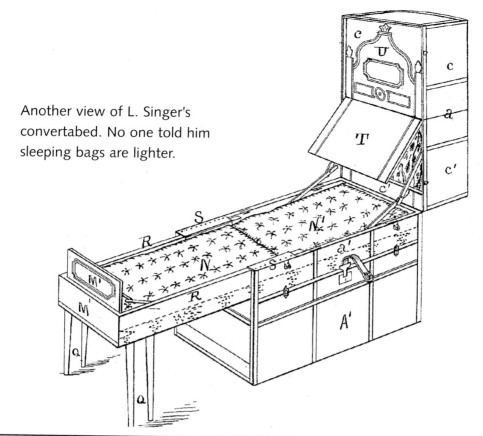

Another view of L. Singer's convertabed. No one told him sleeping bags are lighter.

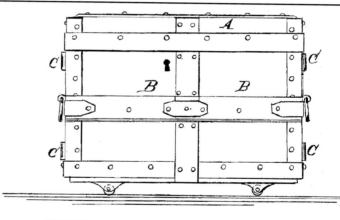

A.L. Mora invented this trunk that has many compartments and drawers in 1868.

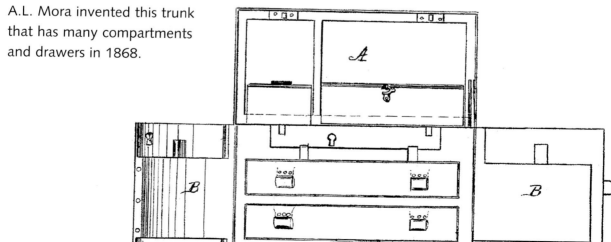

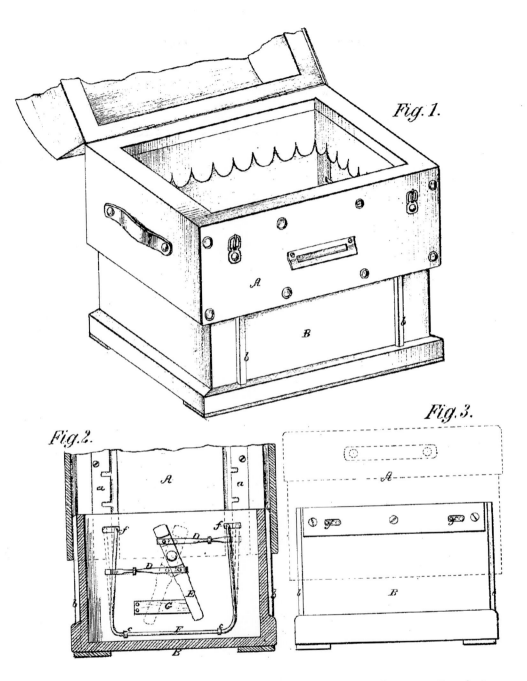

Fig. 1.

Fig. 2.

Fig. 3.

In 1870, James Rice of Middletown, Ind., threw his inventing hat into the telescoping trunk ring with this substantial example.

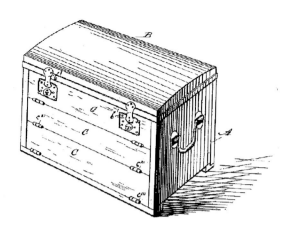

Benoit Bloch of Brooklyn, N.Y.,
came up with this rather
complex dresser trunk in 1880.

Joseph Eno came up with
this version of the wall
trunk in 1880.

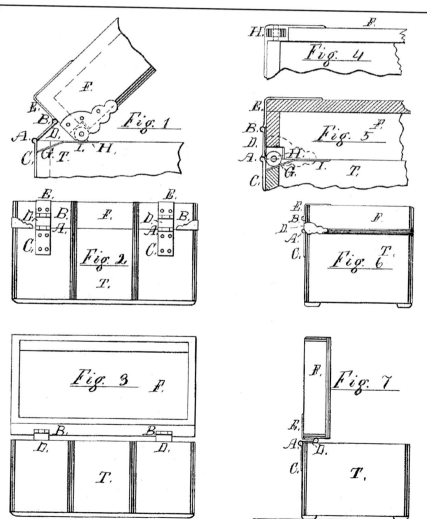

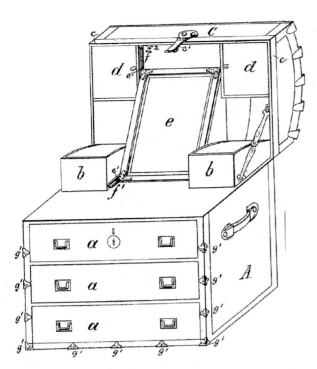

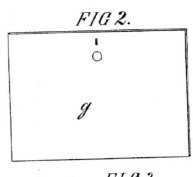

FIG 2.

FIG 3.

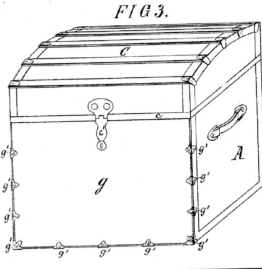

Katie Eubank of Rutherford, Ca., wanted a trunk that was also a bureau. She invented this version in 1887.

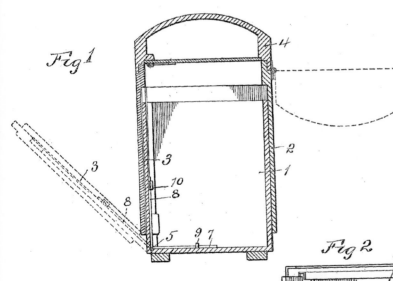

Fig 1

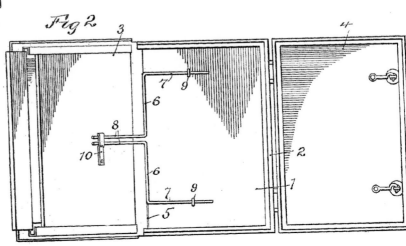

Fig 2

Inventor Mary Hammond of St. Louis, Mo., came up with this sample case that has both a top and front opening. The front door is spring-loaded to prevent it from being soiled by the floor when open.

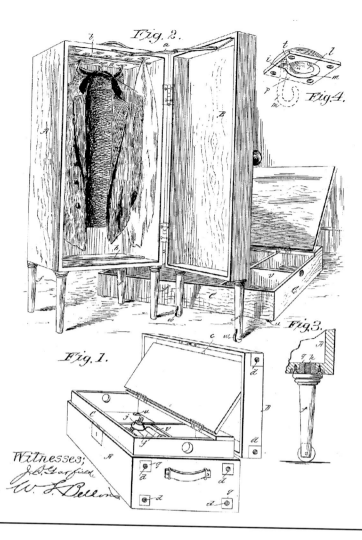

Fig. 2.

Fig. 4.

Fig. 1.

Fig. 3.

Witnesses:
J. A. Garfield
W. L. Belling

Greta L.S. Hayes of Springfield, Mass., invented a convertible wardrobe/trunk in 1891. This trunk can be used either as a wardrobe, or a trunk, depending upon which way it is configured.

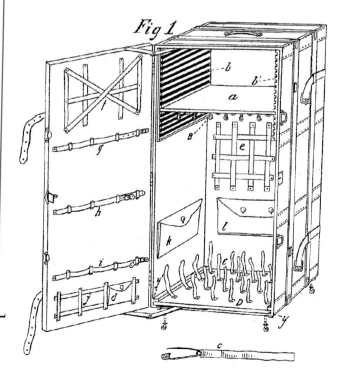

Fig 1

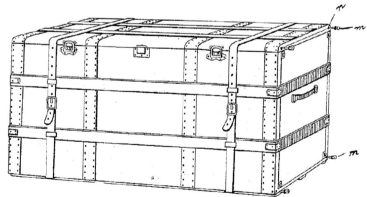

Lizzie Crippen Cozens of Philadelphia, Pa., invented this wardrobe trunk in 1892 in which all the garments would hang separately and be held secure by safety pins. Safety pins?

Antique Trunks

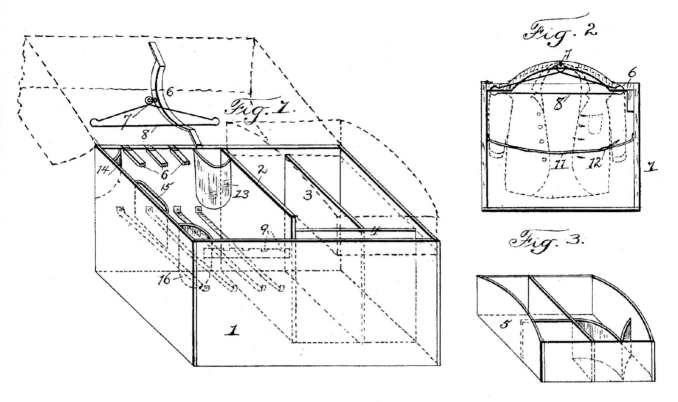

Philomena Yaeger of Helena, Mont., invented this dome top wardrobe trunk in 1892. It's a bit short but perhaps the jackets were too.

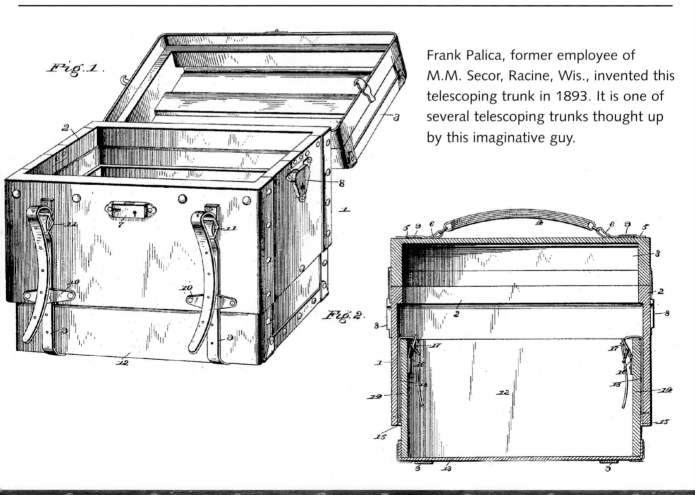

Frank Palica, former employee of M.M. Secor, Racine, Wis., invented this telescoping trunk in 1893. It is one of several telescoping trunks thought up by this imaginative guy.

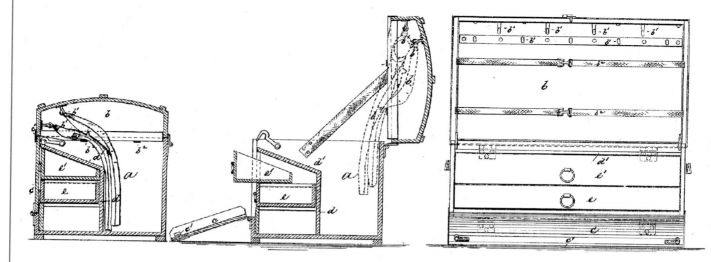

Rudolph Alifield invented this unusual wardrobe trunk in 1894. It has both top and front openings. It is a curved-top trunk with drawers.

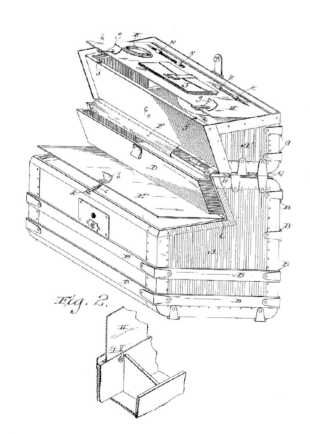

The prolific M.M. Secor produced this wall trunk in 1898.

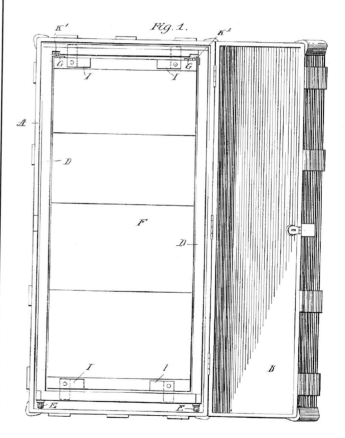

Louis Goldsmith's 1900 wardrobe trunk. Goldsmith of New York, N.Y., invented quite a few trunk innovations.

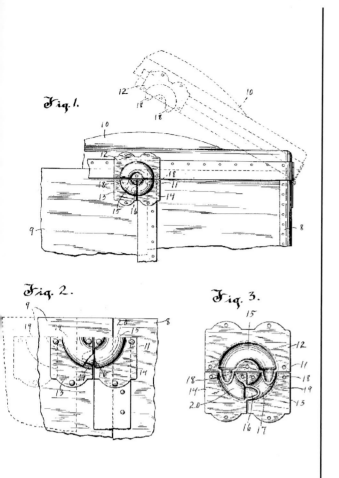

Wheary made many fine wardrobe trunks and this is an improvement on the latching mechanism.

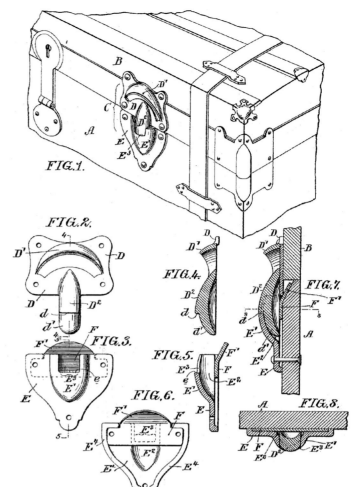

Otto Rangnow of Philadelphia, Pa., invented this handy device in 1904. It is a combination latch/lid lifter. It can be found on many trunks.

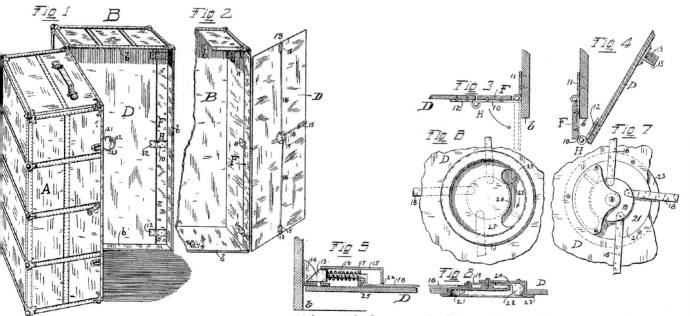

Why settle for a single-folding hinge when you can have a double? Isidor Mendel of Cincinnati, Ohio, invented this double-folder for a wardrobe trunk in 1905.

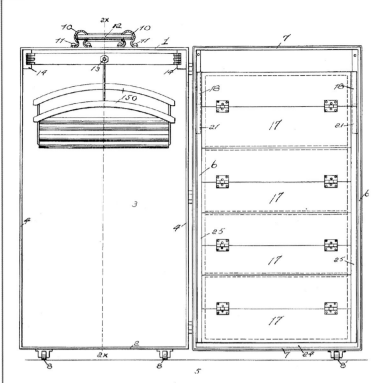

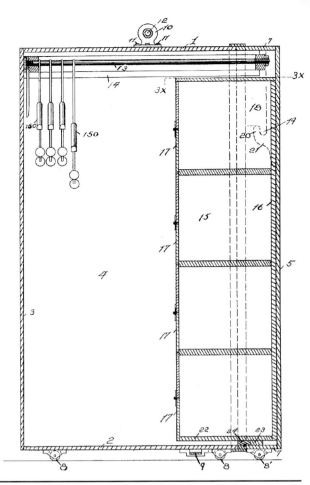

William Likly and John Cannon of Rochester, N.Y., invented a wardrobe trunk in 1907 that had a removable drawer section.

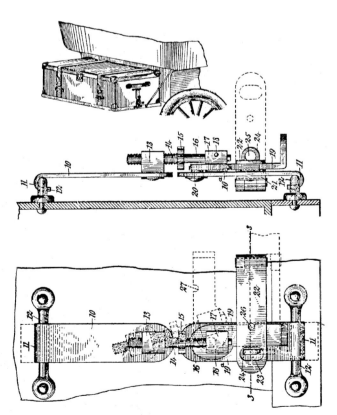

George Loos invented a fastening device for securing trunks to automobiles in 1908.

This wardrobe trunk with the bulbous top was designed so that it couldn't be set down on the top end. It was invented in 1912 by Herman Davis of New Orleans, La.

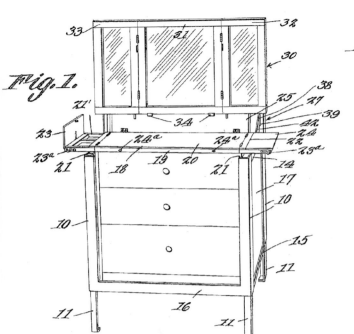

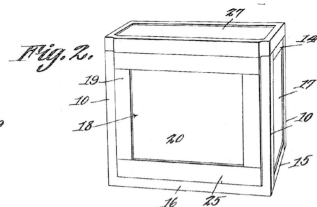

In 1918, Simon Maki of Ishpeming, Mich., invented a homely trunk that could be converted into an even homelier bureau. It must have been a long winter.

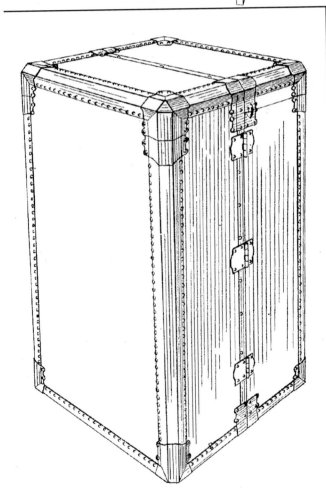

This patent was for the design of a wardrobe trunk issued to Frank Langmuir, Woodbury, N.J., in 1925.

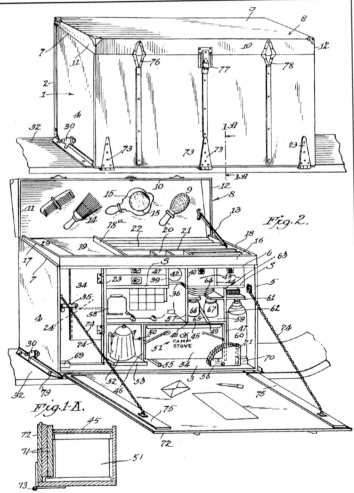

Edward J. McDonald, in 1929, invented this camp kit trunk that has everything from coffeepot to cook stove. It's a Boy Scout's dream.

Advertising

Of course, if you are out for an overnight trip in the Rockies, it's good to carry along a trunk or two with your belongings.

There have been thousands of trunk makers over the years in this country, and some of them even had advertising budgets. But it wasn't until the late 19th or early 20th century that advertising really took off for merchants.

This section provides a look at some of the early 20th century advertisements that were in periodical magazines, newspapers, and even trunk company catalogs.

As you can no doubt tell from some of the descriptions in these ads, the far-reaching slogan is no modern invention.

HARTMANN TRUNKS

BE SURE THE HARTMANN RED ✕ IS ON THE TRUNK YOU BUY

Hartmann Cushion Top WARDROBE TRUNKS

EVERY possible device for ease of operation, convenience and apparel care—they're all in a Hartmann Trunk. But this trunk is not sold on the strength of its visible features—the things you can see. It's sold on the built-in honesty and know-how manufacturing ability that's born of two generations of sincere craftsmen. Sold only by dealers who believe in unusual quality at usual prices.

OVER HALF A MILLION IN USE
QUALITY TELLS

HARTMANN TRUNK COMPANY, *Racine, Wisconsin*
M. Langmuir Manufacturing Company, Ltd., Toronto
Licensed Canadian Manufacturers
J. B. Brooks & Co., Ltd., Great Charles St., Birmingham, Eng.
Licensed Distributors for Great Britain

© 1925, by Hartmann Trunk Co.

ESTABLISHED 1888

Duluth Trunk Co

MORITZ - LAMIE & MORITZ

214 WEST SUPERIOR ST.

DULUTH, MINN.

INNOVATION

TRADE MARK

FROM
TRUNK
OF TREE
TO
TRAVELING
TRUNK

DEMI OR HALF SIZE
SIMPLIFIED INNOVATION

Made in Four Grades
Size 45 x 20 x 15
Drawers 7½ in. deep

$25.00 $45.00 $65.00 $75.00

ELEGANT STEEL-LINED
LEATHEROID TRUNKS
For Bon Ton Travelers.

The Lightest, Strongest and Cheapest Trunks on this Earth!

Used by the leading **Merchants** and **Express Co's** of the **United States**. They will last a lifetime. Most appropriate **Wedding Gift**. We deliver **FREE** in all sections **East** of the **Rocky Mountains**, also in **Great Britain**.

A prominent Washington lady, wife of a leading congressman, writes: "The trunk is a marvel of lightness and strength."

You **Cannot Afford to Use any Other**. Send for Illustrated Lists.

LEATHEROID MFG. CO., Kennebunk, Me.

THE BEALS AND SELKIRK TRUNK COMPANY.

MANUFACTURERS OF HIGH GRADE TRUNKS, BAGS AND CASES.

E. M. DAVIS, President.
J. E. SELKIRK, Vice Pres.
E. H. DAVIS, Treasurer.
PAUL E. DAVIS, Secretary.

SALES AND STOCK ROOMS,
NEW YORK – 558 BROADWAY.
DENVER – CHARLES BLDG.
SAN FRANCISCO – PACIFIC TRUNK & BAG CO.

Wyandotte, Mich April 15th, 1909.

C. Sautter,
Utica, N.Y.

H. B. PITNER,

MANUFACTURER OF

Safety Trunk Guards

Buffalo, Feby 24 1896

John G. Manahan

❖ EVERYTHING FOR TRAVELERS. ❖

ESTABLISHED 1840.

Geo. B. Bains & Sons

Manufacturers

Trunks, Bags, Pocket Books

1028 CHESTNUT STREET

Geo. B. Bains, Jr., Manager,

Philadelphia, *Dec. 31* 190 2

Sold to *Mrs. W. Hinkle Smith*

2025 Locust St

10-02

BILLS NET. DUE WHEN RENDERED.

2936-5

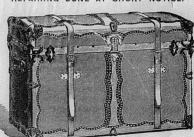

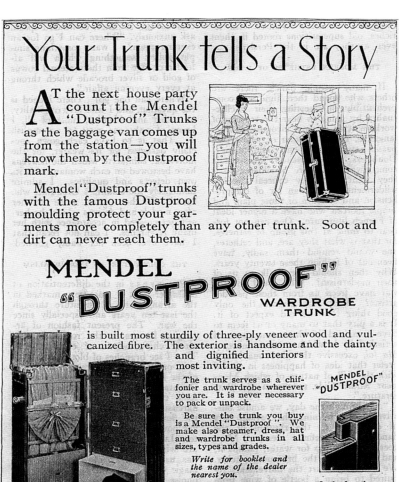

No. 1601.

The A. B. C. of Traveling

A place for everything—everything in its place, where you can get at it without trouble.

Our No. 145 shown below—**the A. B. C. Wardrobe Trunk**—is the most practical trunk of its kind made. It does away with unpacking when you arrive and packing up when you leave—your clothes hang up just as they do in your wardrobe at home—an oak follower keeps them free from wrinkles, When closed takes up only half the floor space of the ordinary trunk. Price $35 and up.

The A. B. C. No. 1601 Automatic Trunk

Raise the lid and you raise the upper tray; drop the front and the second tray slides in and out; easy access to everything.

No. 145.

Style No. 1601, like cut, $20.00.

Write for our book, "Tips to Travelers," telling you more about the A. B. C. Wardrobe Trunk, and showing you many new and practical articles of traveling equipment manufactured by us.

Abel & Bach Company
Largest Makers of Trunks and Bags in the World

Milwaukee, Wis., U. S. A.
Chicago Salesrooms: 46-48 Adams St.

Insist upon having this mark on any Trunk, Suit Case or Bag you buy. It is your guarantee of quality, style and durability.

L½ - OCT 4 1906

Stallman's Dresser Trunk

Easy to get at everything without disturbing anything. No fatigue in packing and unpacking. Light, strong, roomy drawers. Holds as much and costs no more than a good box trunk. Hand-riveted; strongest trunk made. In small room serves as chiffonier. C. O. D. with privilege of examination. 2c. stamp for Catalog.

F. A. STALLMAN
55 W. Spring St.,   Columbus, O.

---

69 Years Young

Please remember this. The old-fashioned patience of 1844 is still a habit at our factory. Our trade mark goes on nothing that is the least bit slap-dash in workmanship. That is the main reason why we are today called upon to produce the widest line of luggage in America.

During our career as the oldest wholesale baggage makers in America we have brought out many innovations. We were the pioneers in producing feather-weight luggage. We originated the leather-bound trunk with canvas-covered sides. Our designers are still setting the pace in luggage.

Buying luggage without first seeing our catalog is a good deal like spelling an unfamiliar word without first consulting the dictionary.

The new wrinkle in this "Likly" Wardrobe Trunk is *no* wrinkles. No matter how rudely it is jostled about, your clothes come out uncrumpled. No fussy folderols. The "Likly" single strap follower keeps everything at your finger-tips. Whichever garment you want comes out in a jiffy. Foundation box is basswood. Covering and interlining is heavy, waterproof Army duck. Rawhide binding. Bronze-steel corner caps and bottom protectors. Ball-bearing rollers. Carries 15 to 18 suits or gowns of average weight. Models for men. Models for women. Prices $70.00 to $75.00. (Add $5.00 to these prices west of the Mississippi.)

One hundred other wardrobe trunks are shown in our catalog. Prices begin at $25.00. Send for a copy.

(No. 61. Wardrobe Trunk)

Victorian Prints

High-styled Jenny Lind trunks are a nice place to keep your treasures.

The Victorian prints in this book have all come from antique trunks. Over the years we have come across many trunks that had a print or two in them. These prints were put into the trunks by the makers as an added feature, decorating the interior lids, trays and compartments.

Whenever we worked on a trunk that had a print inside we would carefully remove the print, scan it into our computer, and restore it. Although time-consuming and tedious, this process was well worth the outcome, because over the years, we have built a substantial collection of full-color Victorian prints that are not available anywhere else.

About Makers

Trunks are a very useful place to keep your toys. A trunk like this can hold up to 600 blocks, 800, if they are stacked neatly.

Over the years, there have been many thousands of trunk makers, both large and small, from one-man shops to factories that employed hundreds of people at their peak. The quality of trunks they turned out ranged from flimsy to fine. The look ranged from just plain ugly to exquisite. For many of the smaller makers, trunks were just one aspect of their business. They made bags, harnesses and tack for horses, boxes, and some made shoes. They were often involved with making many other things from leather.

One such maker, Holmes, of Boston, Mass., made valises, bonnet boxes, and hat cases, as well as trunks. Another, Bates and Company of Somersworth, N.H., also turned out ladies shoes and boots.

Many makers specialized in certain types of trunks. Atwood and Gould of Virginia made trunks for automobiles. Martin Maier of Detroit, Mich., was known for its sample cases, while McLilley of Columbus, Ohio, made military and society goods, trunks especially fitted for regalia.

As the 19th century progressed, the most prolific trunk makers grew in size and some, like Secor of Racine, Wis., employed hundreds at their peak.

This trunk makers database includes information on trunk makers in America and some in Europe, over the years. It is by no means all inclusive, but it will give an indication of what was happening, and point to the centers of trunk making activity: New York, New England, especially the Boston area, the Midwest including Racine, Wis., and of course, Paris, France.

Often makers attached labels to their trunks and we have included many of those labels in this book. Note: Finding an original maker's label is not that common. We encourage you to preserve any label you find, if at all possible.

Information about their products is included, when known.

Allen, Geo. F
Nos. 23 and 27 Middle Street
Lowell, Massachusetts
Manufacturer of and Dealer in trunks, harnesses, bags, dress suitcases, fur and plush robes, blankets, whips and stable supplies.
Wood dome tops with brass locks.
Ca. 1812-1866

Allen, Otis L.
No. 41 Merrimac Street
No. 68 (formerly 41) Merrimac Street
Lowell, Massachusetts
Manufacturer of Trunks, Doc boxes, Valises & Carpet-Bags.
Also, dealer in Umbrellas, Parasols, Accordions, Violins, Combs, Hair-Work, Perfumery, Jewelry, Band-Boxes, Traveling and Work-Baskets, with a great variety of Fancy Goods.
1845

American Trunk Co.
Newark, New Jersey
Flat top steamers, large with fancy brass locks.

Andretti Trunk Co.
San Francisco, California
Eagle trademark trunks.

Atkins, Charles
Tremont St.
Boston, Massachusetts

Atkinson & Long MFG Co. (see The Inshured)
Wardrobes

Atkinson, John S.
48 Fairfield Ave
Bridgeport, Connecticut
Manufacturer of and dealer in lap robes, trunks, bags, blankets, and general horse furnishings.
Atwood & Gould
Virginia
Autorobe
Wardrobe trunks for automobiles.

Augusta Trunk Factory
763 Broad St.
Augusta, Georgia

B B & B Manufacturing
Allegheny, Pittsburgh, Pennsylvania
Wardrobe, flat top steamers.
1891

Bains, Geo B. & Sons
1028 Chestnut Street
Philadelphia, Pennsylvania
Wardrobe trunks w/Belber hangers, makers of bags and trunks for all types of travel.
1840

Baker, John B. and Co.
150 Tremont Street
Boston, Massachusetts
Saddlery and harness house, sole leather trunks.
1826

Bal, William, Co.
Newark, New Jersey and Philadelphia, Pennsylvania
Bal-Built Trunks (brass tag)

Baldwin & Co.
335 6th Ave.
New York, New York
Trunks & Bags, small steamers.
Brass tags

Bankhardt Baggage
Cincinnati, Ohio

Barnard Brothers Co.
372 Main St.
302 Main St.
Factory 456 Park Ave.
Worcester, Massachusetts
Steamers

Barnum (John T.?)
404 Nicollet Ave.
Minneapolis, Minnesota
Flat top leather covered trunks with all brass appointments. Anchor type handles. Brass makers plate on top. 27"W, 14"H, 16"D.
Manufacturer of and dealer in Trunks, Traveling Bags, Suit Cases, Pocket Books.
Repairing and sample work.
Established 1880.

Bates & Co.
Opposite Depot
Somersworth, New Hampshire
Trunks made expressly for Bates & Co., Leading dealers in Trunks, Boots and Shoes.

Bazar Du Voyage
1 Wall St.
No. 1 Wall Street Corner of Broadway.
New York, New York
Canvas covered flat top steamers. Established 18?

Beals and Selkirk Trunk Company
Wyandotte, Minnesota
Steamers
1900

Becker's Leather Goods Co.
Washington, D.C.

Bee Hive Trunk Factory
see Morrison, Lee

Belber Trunk and Bag Company
Philadelphia, Pennsylvania
Steamers, with hangers, ironing board, shoe box.
Belber Traveling Trunk.
1926

Bell, William
56 Court Street Head of Brattle Street
and 62 Tremont Street
Boston, Massachusetts
Manufacturers of solid leather, boot top, fancy and common trunks. Valises, carpet bags, &c. also ladies bonnet and dress trunks. Trunks repaired on short notice.
1840-1850

Bellton
Colorado
Pat. date. Wardrobes. Four drawers on one side with a hat mold and on the other side, it has clothes racks and a shoe bag. "Hard leather" exterior.
1929

Berry, O.H.
Richmond, Virginia

Besbuilt Trunk Company
Newark, New Jersey

Betterbuilt
(see Butterfield)

Bingham Trunk Co.
Buffalo, New York
Steamer trunks. Triple vulcanized seal.

Binsham Trunks
Buffalo, New York
1930

Blais Frerr
181 Notre Dame
Trois Riveria, Canada
Trunks and suitcases.

Boston Baggage Company, The
Boston, Massachusetts
Goldrobe #11780

Bostwick, Charles Jr.
115 Chapel St.
New Haven, Connecticut
Hand trunks.
1855

Bowker Brothers
11 & 13 Columbia St.
Boston, Massachusetts
Sample Trunks and Cases

Boyd, James
27 Merchants Row
Boston, Massachusetts
Large hide covered curved top stagecoach trunks.
1840

Brainard
434 Main St.
Hartford, Connecticut

Breck, T. & W.
No. 24 North Main Street
Providence, Rhode Island
Trunk Manufacturers.

Brewer-Titchner
E.H. Brewer, owner
Courtland, New York

Brooks and Bidleman & Co.
Toledo, Ohio
Leather covered dome top trunks.

Bryant, John & Alfred
Bath and London, England
Leather Trunks and Portmanteaux, and Mill Board boxes.
19th Century

Biltwell Trunks
New York, New York

Buffalo Trunk MFG
Buffalo, New York

Burr, Robert
Nos. 3 and 9 Hanover St.
Boston, Massachusetts
Large leather covered document boxes.
1845

Burr, William
Congress Street
Boston, Massachusetts
Document Boxes.
1840

Burroughs, George
424 E. Water St.
Milwaukee, Wisconsin
Flat top metal covered steamers with fancy brass locks, heavy cast metal trim and corners. George always signed the inside label that described the company's history.
1893
Burrows
Chicago, Illinois

Butterfield Trunk Company
(see Betterbuilt)
Seattle, Washington
LaBelle Luggage Line. Steamers with compartments in lids and trays.

C&M Trunk and Case Company
New York
Vulcanized Hard Fiber trunks.
1898

Cabe-Bierman Wagon Co
St. Louis, Missouri
Wood tool boxes and cases.

Cadmus', Jeremiah
No. 266 Market Street
Philadelphia, Pennsylvania
Soft top black leather covered 1/2 trunks w/steel bands and large brass buttons, with S. Liebrich lock, Phila. Wholesale, retail. Boot, Shoe, & Trunk manufactory.
1850

Canada Trunk Company
Maple leaf logo

Carlsbad, Ernest Hofman
Flat top steamers, very high quality.

Carmen, Charles
Poughkeepsie, New York
Civil War Era flat tops.

Carson, Pirie, Scott and Company
Madison, Wisconsin
Wabash Ave.
Chicago, Illinois
Fine leather and travel goods of all types.

Casey, W.S.
441 6th Ave.
New York, New York

Casey, M. S.
5th Avenue
New York, New York
Vaudeville trunks.

Cattnach, John Trunks and Leather Goods
23w 45th St.
New York, New York
Importers of German leather trunks and luggage products.
Est. 1835

Cavalier Co.
Chattanooga, Tennessee
Brass tag on the lid tells who gave or received the trunk.

Central Trunk Company
Philadelphia, Pennsylvania
1856

Cherry, M.
New York, New York

Clark, W.S. Co.
Springfield, Massachusetts
Made of basswood.
Cleveland Trunk Co.

Clinton Wall Trunk Co.
Clinton, Massachusetts
Wall trunks.

Colorado Wrinkle Free
Non-Wrinkle Trunk Mfr. Co.
Colorado City, Colorado

Colt, Samuel L.
167 Baltimore Street
Baltimore, Maryland
Manufacturer of trunks of every description for traveling, packing, and domestic use.

Conway
Poughkeepsie, New York

Cooper, George
Humpback leather covered trunks.
1859

Crawford and Whitten
Clarksburg, Ohio

Crestien Trunk Co.
Newark, New Jersey
Wardrobe trunks

Crockett, William
Concord, New Hampshire
Leather covered.
1835

Crouch and Fitzgerald
New York, New York
Dome top leather covered steamers. Low flat top steamers, canvas covered, lots of brass corners.
1839-1870

Cumming & Son
Lord Cockburn St.
Edinburgh
Trunks, Portmanteaus, Brushes, and Baskets.

Cummings, Josiah and Sons
82 Union St.
567 Atlantic Ave.
Boston, Massachusetts
"Hub Fibre" Light steel, Fibre, & Rawhide covered No. 657 & 659, "sole and hub leather trunks made to order."

Cummings Trunk
657 Atlantic Ave.
Boston, Massachusetts

Cushing, Charles
New Bedford, Massachusetts
1900

D (with a lion)
See Drucker.

Davis Trunk Factory
Los Angeles, California
1889-1920

Day, H.T.
Westboro Massachusetts
1873
Excelsior Wall Trunks.

Dennison, E.C. Co.
1024-32 N. High Street
Columbus, Ohio
Makers of fireproof wardrobe trunks (with asbestos).

Dethloff & Co.
Denver, Colorado
Manufacturer of trunks and valises.

Detroit Trunk Co.
Detroit, Michigan
Flat top canvas covered steamer.

Derco Trunk Manufacturing
Los Angeles, California

Devine, P. F.
(see Lowell Trunk Co.)
260 Essex St.
Lawrence, Massachusetts
88 Merrimack St.
Lowell, Massachusetts
Factory at
72 Middlesex St.
Flat top steamers.

Dolittle, M.J.
Burlington, Vermont
Saddler and trunk maker.
1830

Dooley, James
104 Third Ave.
New York, New York
Trunks & Bags &c &c, Cor of Astor Place, Cor of
13th Street.

Downing
Boston, Massachusetts
1819

Doyle Brothers
1845

Drew
England
Wardrobes

Drucker, N.
(see Mendel-Drucker)
Cincinnati, Ohio
Wardrobe trunks.
1920

Duker, H.
Baltimore, Maryland
Dufficy, Thos. and Co. Trunk Manufacturers
Louisville, Kentucky
Flat top steamers.

Duguid Bros.
John B.
Toledo, Ohio
Square trunks, 24"W, 19"D, 17"L.
Wall trunks
Logo is a lion standing on a trunk holding the let-
ter "D" and it says "Beauty and Strength."

Duluth Trunk Company
Duluth, Minnesota
Very high quality bevel top trunks, with compartments.
1880

Dunn, C.J.
No. 68 North Calvert Street
Baltimore, Maryland
Manufacturer of TRUNKS traveling bags, ladies'
satchels, &c.

Eagle Trunk Factory
Schmit Brothers, Proprietors
See Schmit
Oshkosh, Wisconsin
Manufacturers or Trunks, Valises, Traveling Bags,
Ladies Bonnet Boxes, Shawl Straps, etc. Trunks
made to order. Trunks covered with canvas when
ordered. We manufacture the Patent Tray. Best
Article in the Market. Round top leather covered
w/round turning latches. Later became Oshkosh
Trunk Company.
1870

Easter & Winship
Boston, Massachusetts
Small steamers with brass buttons. Handle on top.
1858
Eau Claire Trunk Co.
Eau Claire, Wisconsin
Travelers goods, sample trunks, and cases a spe-
cialty.

Eggeman Duguid & Co.
Toledo, Ohio
Wall trunks.
Flower embossed metal covered trunks.
1885

El Paso Trunk Factory
El Paso, Texas

Elsinger, M. J. & Sohne
Wien, Austria

Enderbrock, F. Trunk Co.
NW corner of 3rd and Felix Streets
St. Joseph, Missouri

Englehart, P.
Cleveland ,Ohio

Eveleigh
Canada's Best half trunks.

Everlast (see Petersburg)

Everwear
Newark, New Jersey
Wardrobes
1930

Excelsior
Philadelphia, Pennsylvania
Oak slat trunks with brass compartments, interior
compartments, and trays.

Excelsior Wall Trunk
Made by H.T. Day
Westboro, Massachusetts
1873

Faber, HG & Sons
Utica, New York
Cloth covered teak wood trunks.
1883

Faxon Co.
Albany and
Schenectady, New York
Feigenbaum Trunk Co
Cleveland, Ohio

Fibreware Specialty Co.
Kennett Square
Pennsylvania
Hercules Trademark

Flimsier, JA
Little Rock, Arkansas

Florida Trunk Manufacturing Company
Jacksonville, Florida

Fondulac Trunk Company
D.C. and J.H. Lang Proprietors.
Fond du Lac, Wisconsin

Fox Brothers Trunk Co.
Houlton, Maine
Standard box trunks with canvas covering.

Fricke, Fred, Trunk maker
5 Chicago Street
Elgin, Illinois
Canvas covered box trunks.

Friedman, B.
282 Fulton St.
Brooklyn, New York

Fuller, H F
Denver, Colorado
Very ornamental trunks, heavy duty trunks.

Gallacher, James A.
Salt Lake City, Utah

Garland, F. V.
St. Paul, Minnesota

Gausepol, E.J. and Company
40 W. Washington Street
Indianapolis, Indiana
Hide covered trunks.

Germuiller, F. Trunk Company
Washington, D.C.
1850

Ghearry, M
5th Ave.
New York, New York
Trunk maker, wicker trunks.
1890

Gillmore, J.C. or Arthur
5th Ave.
18 Fourth Avenue
New York, New York
Steamer and other types of very high quality
trunks. These are on a par with Haskell, Crouch &
Fitzgerald, or Louis Vuitton.

Ginbel Brothers
New York,
Paris
1903-1912

Goldsmith L.& Sons
see Neverbreak
Newark, New Jersey
Neverbreak (brand) small steamers.
Wardrobes and field desk type trunks.

Goyard, Edouard
Paris, France
Very high quality steamer trunks. Made with brass
appointments and other fine materials.
1875

Groel, Nicholas
New York, New York
1860-1890

Gromm, FW Trunk Factory
Denver, Colorado
Sales Room:
935 16th St.
Factory:
1219 16th St.
Flat top steamers.

Groskopf Bros.
95 Canal St.
Grand Rapids, Michigan
Manufacturers and dealers in trunks and traveling
bags.

Guggenheim, Louis
Corner 6th and Grand Ave.
Philadelphia, Pennsylvania
Manufacturer of trunks, satchels and valises.

Haley & Cutter
27 Summer St.
Boston, Massachusetts

Hamel, PH
Manchester , New Hampshire
Wardrobe trunks.

Hampton
Wall trunks, and embossed metal covered trunks.
1896

Hancock, Ebenezer
Northhampton, Massachusetts

Hartmann
Racine, Wisconsin
Vobe steamer, Gibralterized cushion top.
Wardrobe with tag.

Bambergers
Newark, New Jersey
Feb 4, 1913, Aug 3, 1926

Haskell Bros.
J.W.C. Haskell, J.E. Haskell.
13, 15, 17 North Green St.
Tribune Building, Madison & Dearborn Sts.
Factory, Nos.13, 15, 17 North Green St.
Chicago, Illinois
Tin and wood trunks. Flat top steamers. Leather
covered Sample Trunks and Cases Made to Order.
Fine Sole Leather and Traveling Trunks a Specialty.
Elephant's head on the label.

Hathaway, Tho's M.
No. 3 Broad Street
Near the State House. Saddles Trunks. Small
leather covered trunks with bonnet top.

Hayes or Haynes, George S.
Headley & Farmer
New York, New York
Later
Newark, New Jersey
1842

Herkert & Meisel Trunk company
(See Meisel)
Wardrobe trunks.
1924

Hickey, Alex L. & Sons
148 Chestnut St.
Philadelphia, Pennsylvania
Civil War Era style trunks with two brass straps.
Awarded medal at The London World's Fair. 15" x
15" x 16"H.

Hickman Trunk Mfg. Co.

Hill, James R.
No.153 Main St.
Concord, New Hampshire
Manuf of solid leather, boot top, common and
fancy trunks, valises, carpet bags, etc. Also ladies
bonnet and dress trunks.

Hirschfelder & Meaney
36 Battery St.
San Francisco, California

H. L. & E. WKS
Bloomfield, New Jersey

Hodge, Levi W.
Nashua, New Hampshire
Manuf. of saddles, harness, trunks of all kinds,
valises, travel bags etc.

Hofmann, Ernest

Holmes (successor to M'Burney)
25 Tremont Row
Boston, Massachusetts
Travelling (sic) Trunks, Valises, Carpet Bags, Ladies'
Dress and Bonnet Boxes, Hat Cases, Bank, Store
and House Trunks.

Horton R. & Sons
E. Somerville, Massachusetts
Curve top leather covered trunks.

Houstan Trunk Co.

Howell & Son Trunk Makers
New York, New York

Hulbert Bros.
Salt Lake City, Utah
1900

Hunter Trunk & Bag Co.
162 Asylum Street
Hartford, Connecticut.
Flat top green canvas covered steamers with two
trays.

Indestructo Trunk Company
Mishawaka, Indiana
Steamers.
See also: National Veneer.

Innovation Trunk Company
New York
Patent Dec. 28, 1909, Wardrobe trunks.
1909

Jamestown Lounge Company
Jamestown, New York
1888

Jeune, Bertin
Au Depart
29 Avenue de L'Opera
Paris, France

Johnson
1 Main St.
Concord, New Hampshire
Flat top Civil War Era trunks, brown leather covered. Sm brass buttons.
1860

Julian Leather Goods Co

Karri-Keen Mfg. Co
Sioux City, Iowa
Automobile trunks
1926

Keefe, JJ
Boston, Massachusetts
Steamer trunks.

Kellogg & Clark
No. 13 Court Street
Boston, Massachusetts
Harness & Trunk makers, military equipment & c.
Small valise,
1840

Keystone, R & H (see R&H)?
Wardrobe trunks.
1916

Kuettel, Charles
Fresno, California
1915-35

Lagowitc, A.J. Maker
San Antonio, Texas
Alligator embossed metal covered trunks.
1880-1892

Langmuir Manufacturing Company
Matthew Langmuir, Trunk and Luggage makers
Toronto, Canada
Langmuir-Hartmann
Toronto, Canada.
Langmuir hooked up with Hartmann and manufactured Hartmann style cushion top wardrobes.
1910-1955

Lankler, George C.
207 Mail St.
Buffalo, New York
Father made trunks at this address from 1880-1884, then George from 1885-1939.
Flat top steamer trunks.
1880-1939

Leatheroid Manufacturing Co.
Kennebunk, Maine
Very high quality artificial leather trunks.

Libbey, Issac
Rochester, New Hampshire
1834
Lieberman, L.
Atlanta, Georgia

Liebrick, C.
Philadelphia, Pennsylvania
Jenny Lind trunks

Likly, Henry
Rochester, New York
Established 1848
Steamers, Wardrobes
1844

Lorenz, Wm.
Minneapolis, Minnesota
Theatrical trunks

Los Angeles Trunk Factory
228 Southmark Street
Los Angeles, California
Phone Red 2567
Home 1657

Lowell Trunk Manufactory
(see Devine, P.F.)
30-32 Middlesex St.
Lowell, Massachusetts
P.F. Devine, Prop. Dome top steamers. Trunks, Extension Cases, Repairing. Bags, Valises, Fancy leather goods. Old trunks taken in exchange. Pat.
Mar 1884
1884

Lucas, Richard
Portmanteaus, small hide covered curved top document boxes.
18th century.

Luce Trunk Factory
Kansas City, Missouri
Leather covered trunks.

Maas, E
Tremont St.
Boston, Massachusetts
Curved top canvas covered steamers with hardwood slats. Good quality.
1870

Maidrite
Wardrobe trunks #503 Blue
1927

Maier, Martin & Co.
102 Woodward Avenue
Detroit, Michigan
Black trunks with bood trim
"Rite-Hite Trunks"
Wardrobes Pat. 1905-1914
"Full line of SAMPLE TRUNKS professional trunks, sample cases always on hand on the sales room of Martin Maier."
1865

Malm, CA & Company
Bush Street
Sutter Street
San Francisco, California
Trunks, traveling bags, and valises.

Manhatten
Neverbreak, wardrobes

March, Nath'l B.
Daniel (Broad) Street
Portsmouth, New Hampshire
Saddles Bridles Harnesses and Trunks made and constantly kept for sale.
1809-1819

Marshall Field & Co.
Chicago, Illinois
Trunks & Locks.
1906

Mason & Parker MFG Co.
Winchendon, Massachusetts
Durable Toys. Dolls trunks, flat tops with slats and trays.
1900

Mason & Whitehead
225 Brompton Rd.
Trunks, Bag & Brush makers. Trunks repaired or taken in exchange.

Maud, William H.
Salem, Massachusetts
Civil War era type trunks.
1850

McDonald, A.
44 School St.
Boston, Massachusetts
Large leather covered document boxes.
1835

McGee, John
108 North Howard Street
Baltimore, Maryland
Manufacturer of ladies satchels, etc.
Flat top steamers.

McLean, Daniel & Son
New Glasgow, Nova Scotia
Horse on label. Saddle, Collar, and Harness Trunk Manufactory.

McLeod & Shotton
Montreal, Canada

McLeod Hawthorne & Co.
1819 Notre Dame Street
Montreal, Canada
Dealers in travellers requisites generally sample trunks a specialty. Repairing & order work executed with despatch. Trunks & valises. Telephone 1226 Successors to McLeod & Shotton

McLilley & Co.
Columbus, Ohio
Canvas covered trunks, 10.5"h, 18"W, 11"D.
Manufacturers of Military and Society Goods.

Meek, A.E and Company
Denver, Colorado
Steamer trunks.

Meisel Co.
(see also Herkert)
St. Louis, Missouri
Wardrobe trunks.

Mendel Drucker
See Drucker
Cincinnati, Ohio
Wardrobe #94834
High quality wardrobe trunks. "Ideal" brand.
1925

Meyering, J.V
Chicago, Illinois
Wardrobe trunks.

Miller, S.S. and Son
Summer St. and Atlantic Ave.
Boston, Massachusetts

Minson, F.B.
York Town, Virginia
Pine "signature" trunks, F.B. Minson, Maker on
brass plate

MM & Co

M&M
New York
Leather, canvas, metal, wardrobes, dome tops,
etc., High quality, well made trunks.
1860-1930

Mobile Trunk Co
Wardrobes

Molloy, George
15 Market Street
Lowell, Massachusetts
Manufactured and sold by. (Picture of Jenny Lind
trunk on label) Where all kinds of iron, zinc, canvas, duck & cloth trunks may be found cheaper
than at another establishment in Lowell. Every
trunk made by Molloy has on it a lock that the
keys of trunks sold elsewhere will not unlock. Old
trunks taken in exchange for new ones. Trunks
repaired and locks put on at very reasonable
prices.
Locks for sale. Keys fitted to all kinds of locks. Any
pattern or style of trunk desired made to order. No
paper trunks.

Morrison, Lee Co.
see Bee Hive
27 W Washington St.
Indianapolis, Indiana
Bee Hive Trunk Factory

Moseley, David
No. 44 Marlboro Street
Boston, Massachusetts
Saddle Cap Trunk and Harness maker.
Curved top stagecoach trunks.
1835

Moyer, Thomas
38 Market St.
Philadelphia, Pennsylvania
Leather covered three part
trunks. High quality.
1840
Moynat Trunk

EDWARD P. MOYER,
SADDLE, BRIDLE,
HARNESS & TRUNK
MANUFACTURER,
Nos. 18 & 150 Market Street,
Sign of Golden Saddle No. 38,
PHILADELPHIA.

Multnomah
Portland, Oregon
Wardrobe Patented 3/8/21
1921

Murphy's
St. Louis, Missouri
The best baggage built.
Wardrobe trunks.

National Veneer Products Company
Mishawka, Indiana
Indestructo Trunk #A5284
1903

Nathans, Samuel Inc.
Theatrical Trunks.

Neat, Nathan
566 Washington Street
Boston, Massachusetts
1825

Neverbreak
see Goldsmith and Son

Nevercrack

New England Trunk Company
Wardrobes

Non-wrinkle Trunk Manufacturing Co.
Colorado City, Colorado

Northwestern Trunk Co.
248 Nicollet Ave.
Minneapolis, Minnesota
Flat top canvas covered steamers.
1900

Oak Hill Company
Fitchburg, Massachusetts
Doll trunks.

Oshkosh Trunk Company
Madison and Oshkosh, Wisconsin
Suitcases, wardrobe trunks. 1915, The Chief
1913-1923

Overland Trunk Company
New York

P&S
Trunks that wear everywhere, registered trademark.

Pacific Trunk and Bag Company
San Francisco, California
1900

Palica, FJ Co.
Racine, Wisconsin
Palica's Celebrated Trunk on a plate.
Also, alligator embossed metal covered steamers.
1872

Palmer
Salt Lake City, Utah

Perry, E. and Co.
A prize medal at Paris exposition of 1867. Highest
honor of any American trunk maker.
1867

Peterkin, G. E.
Aberdeen, Scotland

Petersburg Trunk Company
Petersburg, Virginia
Makers of Everlast trunks, wardrobe style

Phillips Trunk Factory
50 3rd St.
Camel top steamers.

Pigny Freres
Toulouse, France

Plant, John LTD
Derby & Burton-on-Trent, England
Wardrobes
"Watajoy" London, England

Preismeyer Brothers
Theatrical trunk, large, 48x27x30.

Pueblo Trunk Company
Pueblo, Colorado
Canvas covered flat top steamers.

R&G Everwear Trunks
(See Rauchbagh, Goldsmith)

R&H Modern Trunks
(see Keystone)?
Steamers.

Rashkin, E.
Between Bedford & Nostrand Ave.
Brooklyn, New York
Trunks, Leather goods, Umbrellas, and Pocket
Books. Also keys & locks made & set. Tel Lafayette
6546

Rauchbagh, Goldsmith Co. (see R&G)

Reading Trunk Factory
302 Penn Street
Reading, Pennsylvania
High quality flat top canvas covered steamers.
Brass Yale lock, cast iron fancy end caps and
latches.
1895

Reed, W. S. Toy Co.
Leominster, Massachusetts
Solid brass lock, two trays, casters, 2 secret com-
partments.

Rescousie, A.
S.W. Corner 42nd St. & 8th Ave.
New York, New York
Manufacturer and Dealer in Trunks and Bags.
Dome top steamer.

Reynolds, E.D.
Fremont Street
Portland, Maine
Trunk and Bag Manufacturer. Label shows a man
with his mouth open and the company name in
his mouth.
1800

Rice, Horace
No. 30 Hanover Street
Boston, Massachusetts
Small black leather covered document boxes.
Saddles, Harnesses, Caps, & Trunks. Near Earls
Coffee House. Old Trunks Taken.
1840

Rockford Trunk and Leather Company
Rockford, Illinois

Rogers and Madison Trunk Corp
Petersburg, Virginia
3 Genuine Ply.

Roos
Sweetheart Cedar Chest.

Rose Company

Rountree, HW and Bros Trunk and Bag Co.
Richmond, Virginia
Pittsburgh, Virginia
Roller tray trunks. Wardrobes, Steamers.
Royal Line of Guaranteed Goods.
1889-1914

Rubin, Max & Sons
New York, New York

Saratoga Trunk Company
Saratoga, New York
1865

Sawyer, Asa
Corner of Your & Exchange St.
Bangor, Maine
Manufacturers of harness, saddles, trunk valises, &
carpet bags. Wholesale, retail. Repairing executed
with despatch.

SBT Co.
Finely made dome top steamers with lots of very
fancy hardware and slat clamps. SBT Co on cast
iron clamps. Crystalized finish, five front to back
top slats, two side to side top slats, five vertical
front slats, double embossed lock patent dated
October 1871, 31"W, 27"H, 20"D.
1871

Schaulie, Fred Trunk Co.
Louisville, Kentucky
36x23x36.

Schmit (Bros) Trunk Company

The Schmit Trunk Company
See Eagle Trunk Factory
Oshkosh, Wisconsin
Travel Well Trunks, Wardrobe trunks, black com-
position covering.
1910

Schwartz Brothers Trunk and Bag Manufactory.
281 Fulton
New York, New York

Secor, M.M.
Racine, Wisconsin
Wall trunk, Pat. Jan 2, 1894
During their peak they had 250 employees turning out 80,000 trunks per year.
1861

Seward Trunk and Bag Co.
Petersburg, Virginia
Wonderrobes, Pat. Pending

Shelton & Cheever
7 Washington Street
58 Brattle Street
Boston, Massachusetts
Early small document boxes.
1835

Shilling, R. L.

Shilling, Howard & Co.
Indiana

SHR & Co.
Dome top trunks.

Shwayder
Denver/Detroit, Colorado
 "Sampson" trunks.

Spear, James M.
311 Fulton St. Cor Johnson Under Tiee's Jewelry Store
Brooklyn, New York
Taylors celebrated patent trunks and all other styles. Fancy and Traveling Bags of every description and quality. Trunks repaired. Steamers.
Siemonds, James

Sotco Trunk Co.
New York, New York
Curve top trunks with brass tags.
1890

Spaulding National Trunk Corp.
Wardrobes.

Springfield Trunk Company
The Original Trunk
1886

St Paul Trunk Co.
St. Paul, Minnesota
1879
Dome top flower embossed metal covered trunk.

Stallman's Dresser Trunks
East Spring Street
Columbus, Ohio

Stallman, Frank A.
Theatrical and Commercial Work.
Short steamers.
Opens from the front with drawers.

Standard Trunk Factory, The
Wardrobes upright and opens with drawers on one side and a clothes rod, wooden hangers, and an ironing board, and a small carry case on the other side.

Standwell
Philadelphia, Pennsylvania
Wardrobe trunks.

Stark (Koffer)
Wardrobe trunks.

Starr, C.R. Co.
Columbus, Ohio
Camel back trunks.

Starr , John C.
2629-21-23 First Avenue
Seattle, Washington.
Manufacturer of Fiber and Metal Trunks.
Strongest Trunks Manufactured.
Sterling Trunk Company

Stiles Brothers
New York, New York
1858

Stromburg & Kraus
Wardrobes.

Sweester, Benjamin
Portsmouth, New Hampshire
Trunkmaker, Saddler.
1803-1833

Tappan, Amos
11 State St.
Newburyport, Massachusetts

Taylor, CA Trunk Works
39 East Randolph St.
130 West Madison St.
Chicago, Illinois
1438 Broadway
New York, New York
Makers of the celebrated Taylor XX professional
trunks
Taylor made very high quality trunks.
Other addresses:
28 East Randolph
Chicago, Illinois
657 West Madison
131 West 38th Street
New York, New York
1890

The Inshured Trunk
(see Atkinson & Long)
New York, New York
7469 Reg. US Pat Office, Wardrobe trunks.

Topham Trunk Co.
Washington, D.C.
Field Trunk. Opens to desk, ca. 1890.
1855

Tronic-Mackensie
Metal covered trunks with brass locks.

Tuerke Baggage Builders
Baltimore, Maryland
Trunk and leather store.

Union Supreme Trunk and Bag

United States Trunk Company

Fall River, Massachusetts
Large steamer trunks.

US Trunk
Cardboard.
1920

Vanderman Manufacturing
Willimantic, Connecticut
Metal covered steamers manufactured for the
mining and railroad industries and other heavy
duty uses.
2.Hand forged of steel with oak staves, hand riv-
eted to the trunk. Stamp indicated it held tools
for a water tube boiler manufactured by
Edgemore Iron Works, Edgemore, Delaware.
18"x 24"x 12".
1897

Virginia Trunk and Bag
Petersburg, Virginia
Wardrobes, Genuine Vulcanized Hard Fibre.
Fell 125 feet without damage.

Vogler & Geudtner
210-212 Madison and 197 N. Wells
Chicago, Illinois
Herman Vogle

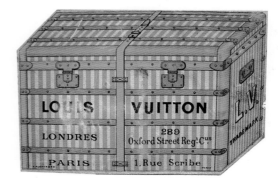

Vuitton, Louis
Paris, London
Makers of all types of very high quality luggage.
1854

W.F.Peake
Chattanooga,Tennessee
Dome top steamers.
1880

Walsh, C. & Son

Walsh, Harry
466 Broadway
Albany, New York
Tel 914 Dealer In trunks & bags. Manufacturers of
fine harness.

Wardrola

Warren and Note
Woodstock, Vermont
Harness And Trunk Makers
Wesley & Johnson
New Haven, Connecticut

Wesson & Valley
No. 2 North Main St.
Providence, Rhode Island
Document Boxes.
1840

Whalen, New Jersey
Manchester, New Hampshire
Alligator embossed dome top steamers.
Harness and trunk man.

Wheary Trunk Co.
Empire State Building
New York, New York
Wardrobes, suitcases.

Wheary-Burge Trunk Co.
Racine, Wisconsin
Wardrobes.

Wheelock, James
Worcester, Massachusetts
Jenny Lind, leather covered with large brass buttons.
1850
Whitney, G. U.

Whittel Trunk & Bag Company
Knoxville, Tennessee
Cedarobe, wardrobe trunks.
1880

Wichita Trunk Factory
MFGS of Veneer Trunks and Sample Work

Wilkins Trunk Co.
Dallas, Texas

Williams & Co.
London, England
Basket trunks.

Wilmot, Alonzo
Cohoes, New York
Black leather covered trunks, curved tops.
34, 18, 18.
1860

Wilt, Chas T.
40 E. Madison St.
Michigan Ave.
180 Wabash Street
Chicago, Illinois
Wardrobe trunk, dark green ca.1912
Humpback, large
Patent Aug 26, 1876
Bridal trunk, camel back dated 1862 on liner.
1862-1912

Winship, Harry A.
(see Winship, W.W.)
16 Treamont St
Boston, Massachusetts
d. 1909. After Harry died his nephew William
Winship took over the company and renamed it
WW Winship. He owned and operated the company from 1909-1918
1876

Winship, W.W.
(see Winship, H.A.)
7 Elm Street
Boston, Massachusetts
Steamers. High quality.
1884

Wirsing, CH

Wyatt, A-B
Sanbornton Bridge, New Hampshire
Mfg. of & dealer in harnesses, trunks, valises, carpet bags, collars, bridles, whips, etc.

Young, Homer Company
Toledo, Ohio
Wall trunks and Dresser trunks. A flat top steamer with fold up front and has drawers that slide out the front.

Zinc Co.
Illinois

Sources

The following is a list of resources including trunks, books, parts, and other information. This list includes a brief summary of what the company offers and contact information.

The Trunk Shop
62 Canaan Back Road
Barrington, NH 03825
(877) 878-6588
Web site: http://www.trunk.com
Summary:
The country's premier source for fine antique trunks, sells and refinishes antique trunks of all types. We sell trunk parts and publish an in-depth refinishing book.
Trunks
Refinishing service
Parts
Refinishing Book

Armand's Antique Trunks
Web site: www.armandstrunks.com
Summary:
We offer custom refinishing services as well as our own quality refinished antique trunks.
Trunks
Refinishing services

Pittsburgh Antique Trunks
Web site:
http://home.attbi.com/~lvhs2000/trunk/sale.htm
Summary:
We buy, sell and refinish antique trunks. Superior quality, workmanship and reasonably priced.
Trunks
Refinishing services

Talbot's Trunks
Hal and Careen Talbot
Depot Antique Gallery in Bouckville, N.Y.
(315) 687-9498
Web site: http://www.talbotstrunks.com
Summary:
We restore all kinds of trunks, which date prior to 1900. We refinish the exterior, usually removing the outer covering, and line the interiors with coordinating fabrics. We restore for people who own trunks and also sell restored trunks retail.
Trunks
Refinishing services

This Old Trunk
(615) 867-2060
Web site: www.ThisOldTrunk.com
Summary:
Offer a variety of professionally restored or original condition antique trunks. Specialize in early and rare styles including Jenny Linds, Theatricals, Saratogas, etc.
Trunks

Treasured Chests
Web site: http://www.oldtrunks.com
Summary:
Antique Trunk Restoration, Yours or Ours. Treasured Chests has specialized in research, restoration, and sales of antique trunks since 1972.
Trunks
Refinishing services

Antique Trunks

Brettuns Village Trunks & Leather
Churchill Barton
P.O. Box 772
Auburn, ME 04212
(207) 782-7863
Web site: http://www.brettunsvillage.com
Summary:
Old Trunks, New Leather, Parts
Trunks
Refinishing service
Parts

Pecksprimitives.com
Point Pleasant, NJ 08742
30 years experience in the trunk refinishing business.
Trunks
Refinishing

US patent Web site:
http://www.uspto.gov/go/classification/uspc190/sched190.htm
Class 190 is the patent office designation for trunks.

Some trunks were even useful for carrying the family pets.

Glossary

Bevel top: the front and back of the top on this trunk have an angular bevel rather than being curved or 90 degrees.

Circa: The term "circa" means around this time. That is, circa 1875 would mean around 1875, give or take a few years. The abbreviation for circa is ca.

Civil War Era: any trunk made during the Civil War Era.

Curved-sided: used to describe the front and back of a Jenny Lind style trunk.

Curved-top: where the top has a curve from front to back.

Document box: an earlier, smaller container that looks much like trunks of the era except that they usually had one small handle on top.

Dome top: where the top rises to a peak from all four sides. Also called camel back or hump back.

Embossed metal: the covering of the trunk in a thin sheet of metal, stamped with a design such as leaves or alligator pattern.

Half trunk: a trunk that is about half as wide as a standard trunk. Sometimes called a hat trunk.

Hide-covered: the covering of the trunk is untanned hide with the hair still on.

Low profile: a trunk like this would be a full sized steamer trunk with the exception that it is only about one-half the height.

Stagecoach: another term for an early trunk, which may also be hide covered or leather covered.

Steamer: a style of trunk made after 1870, or so.

Straight-side: used to describe the front and back of a Jenny Lind style trunk.

Wardrobe: this trunk stands on end and has hangers on one side and drawers on the other.

Index

Index